CLEAN &
SIMPLE

The Old Farmer's Almanac Home Library

CLEAN & SIMPLE

A Back-To-Basics Approach to Cleaning Your Home

Christine Halvorson & Kenneth M. Sheldon

AND THE EDITORS OF

The Old Farmer's Almanac

OLD FARMER'S ALMANAC HOME LIBRARY
Series Editor: Sarah Elder Hale
Consulting Editor: Susan Peery
Copy Editor: Barbara Jatkola
Design and Layout: Sheryl Fletcher
Design Consultant: Karen Savary
Cover Illustration: Sara Love

LIBRARY OF CONGRESS CATALOGING-IN-PUBLICATION DATA
Halvorson, Christine.
Clean & simple : a back-to-basics approach to cleaning your
home /by Christine Halvorson & Kenneth M. Sheldon, and the
editors of the Old farmer's almanac. p. cm. -- (The old farmer's
almanac home library) Includes index.
ISBN 0-7370-0040-6 (alk. paper)
1. House cleaning. I. Sheldon, Kenneth M. II. Old farmer's
almanac. III. Title. IV. Title: Clean and simple. V. Series.
TX324.H35 1999
648'.5--dc21 98-46571 CIP

Distributed in the book trade by Time-Life Books, Inc.

TIME-LIFE BOOKS IS A DIVISION OF TIME LIFE INC.

TIME-LIFE CUSTOM PUBLISHING
Vice President and Publisher: Terry Newell
Vice President of Sales and Marketing: Neil Levin
Director of Acquisitions: Jennifer Pearce
Director of Special Markets: Liz Ziehl
Editor: Linda Bellamy

TIME-LIFE is a trademark of Time Warner Inc. U.S.A.

Contents

Foreword

I USUALLY CLEAN MY HOUSE EVERY SATURDAY MORNING, and although my husband and children are willing to help (and I'm quick to enlist them), I am the person in my family who seems to accept the most responsibility for making the house clean and tidy. I love to sit down with a cup of tea when I'm finished and simply enjoy the pure, suspended feeling of being in a clean, uncluttered space.

It doesn't last long. Nature abhors a vacuum — and she doesn't think much of vacuum cleaners either. Family, friends, pets, newspapers, cookie crumbs, laundry, and dirty dishes materialize within minutes. The old Greek myth about the hopeless task of cleaning the Augean stables comes to mind. Oh, well, there's always next Saturday.

The authors of this book appreciate both the love of cleanliness and the resistance to achieving it. They also know that the simple approach — liberal use of old standby cleaners such as salt, lemon juice, vinegar, and baking soda — is quick, effective, and frugal.

Saving time, effort, and money is something that the founder of *The Old Farmer's Almanac*, Robert B. Thomas, would have heartily endorsed, I think. Thomas (1766–1846), who published the first edition of the Almanac in the fall of 1792, concerned himself mostly with the farmer's relentless rounds — haying, shearing, worming, culling, harrowing, hauling, winnowing, cutting, digging, mucking — but he did drop in the occasional piece of advice about taking care of the house.

In the 1794 edition, Thomas offered "a cheap, easy, and clean mixture for effectually destroying bed bugs." This potion, involving wine, turpentine, and "camphire" (camphor), was to be liberally sponged onto the bedstead or furniture. Thomas promised that it would "neither soil, stain, nor in the least hurt, the finest silk or damask habits." A frugal Yankee to the core, he also reminded people that once the bed was bugless, they should retire early to save on wood and candles.

The next year, 1795, Thomas published an article titled "Method of Taking Out Spots of Ink, from Linen." He noted that this method was even better than using lemon juice, which could "corrode" the linen. He advised dipping the ink spot in melted wax or purified tallow, then washing the item as usual. I can't help but wonder whether Mrs. Thomas (Hannah Beaman Thomas) was the real source of this tip. Her husband no doubt spattered many an ink drop onto his linens in the course of calculating and writing his Almanac. And it's fairly safe to assume that it was Hannah who did the weekly laundry.

Since those early editions of the Almanac, we've regularly published articles and tips on housekeeping and fielded countless letters and telephone calls (and lately e-mail) from readers who want to know the best (quickest, easiest, cheapest) way to clean, polish, freshen, and maintain their homes. We're happy to have this book available now as a compendium of practical solutions to many of the vexing problems that beset us around the house, from dust bunnies and static cling to spotty mirrors and smelly sponges. I, for one, will use the book a lot — especially on Saturday mornings.

SUSAN PEERY
Managing Editor
The Old Farmer's Almanac

Introduction

It is of the utmost importance in the life of a farmer as it is in that of every other man, to make home attractive, not merely to the stranger, but to all the family. Order and neatness in all the domestic arrangements will, of course, conduce largely to this end. No dwelling can have the air of comfort, and cheerfulness, and thrift, without this essential condition.
— The Old Farmer's Almanac, 1876

*I*N OUR MOTHERS' DAY, CLEANING WAS BASICALLY WOMEN'S work. But times have changed. Now fewer families have someone at home full-time to keep track of household tasks. We have lots of fancy tools and equipment for cleaning but less time to use them. When it comes to commercial cleaning products, there are so many options we have no idea what to use where.

Because Mom did all the cleaning, some of us never learned to do it properly. Then came college, where we were able to pass off cleaning tasks to our roommates, ignore them entirely, or find someone who needed a term paper typed in exchange for doing the laundry. Unfortunately, Cleaning 101 wasn't a graduation requirement, so many of us took it pass/fail and failed.

Marriage was a rude awakening, especially for those of us who expected to marry someone who knew all the cleaning tricks we didn't. We imagined there were people out there who actually enjoyed cleaning and did it well, and we just had to find them. Boy, were we wrong.

So where does that leave us? We're cleaning impaired, too busy, and can't see the point of most cleaning tasks. Why bother cleaning something that's just going to get dirty again? (According to a government-funded survey, a kitchen counter devoid of dirty dishes remains clean for approximately 17 seconds.) Furthermore, cleaning is a thankless job. It's boring and repetitive and doesn't pay. And Mom is no longer around to help. The situation is desperate.

Fortunately, over the years *The Old Farmer's Almanac* has preserved cleaning wisdom passed down from mothers, grandmothers, and great-grandmothers. We've culled those old Almanacs (more than 200 years' worth) to find the best cleaning tips, along with some amusing, antiquated, and (to modern sensibilities) downright strange ideas. The recipes for our HomeMade cleaning products, which appear throughout the book, are guaranteed to save you money and clean just as well as the commercial products. We've also included tips that help to reduce the time you spend cleaning, increase your efficiency, and cut down on cleaning tasks, and we offer our own bits of wit and wisdom to lighten and brighten your cleaning burdens.

Mom would be proud.

This symbol appears throughout the book accompanied by a piece of cleaning advice from a past edition of *The Old Farmer's Almanac*. The year of the particular edition, in parentheses, follows the advice.

Chapter 1
Basic Training

*T*HIS IS A BOOK ABOUT CLEANING. IF YOU'RE LIKE US, CLEANING IS right up there with elective surgery and reconciling your checkbook when it comes to having fun. Given that, we've written this book with a few simple principles in mind.

Real people can clean. Some books on cleaning present an approach that makes Martha Stewart look like a lazy goof-off. Fear not. We aren't cleaning fanatics, just two people who want to get the job done.

Cleaning doesn't have to be complicated. You don't need a supermarket full of commercial products and high-tech cleaning tools. With a few simple ingredients and basic tools you can achieve domestic cleanliness.

Cleaning can be fun. All right, maybe *fun* is too strong a word. How about less painful than watching your neighbor's video of his trip to Arizona? At any rate, we've tried to highlight the lighter side of cleaning throughout this book.

Of course, your attitude about cleaning will depend largely on your cleaning personality. Before we begin discussing how to clean various areas of the home, let's take a closer look at the various cleaning personalities.

DEFINING YOUR CLEANING PERSONALITY

Lately, bestseller lists seem beset by self-help books with titles like *The Mythic Inner Life of Highly Effective Men Who Run with Women from Venus and the Inner Children Who Love Them but Are Afraid to Ask*. Despite its commitment to time-tested, tried-and-true wisdom, *The Old Farmer's Almanac* also is mindful of the need to stay abreast of current trends. To that end, we asked a well-known research firm, the Ersatz Institute of Ethnological Influences Organization (EIEIO), to provide us with the following analysis of cleaning personality types.

THE AVOIDANCE CLEANER

Each of us has some cleaning chores we dislike, such as washing dishes, vacuuming, or cleaning the toilet. But the Avoidance Cleaner has a particular task she hates so much that she'll do anything to put it off — even other cleaning tasks. Avoidance Cleaners can actually get a lot of work done, all the while hoping the dishes will somehow magically wash themselves. As a stimulus for cleaning, guilt isn't the best motivation, but it isn't bad. If you're an Avoidance Cleaner, just take care of the things you can handle yourself, then hire someone (or bribe your kids) to do the chores you hate. Or use paper plates.

THE HARRIED-HOST CLEANER

This is the person who cleans only when company is coming. Suddenly, all the papers, projects, and half-read books that covered every flat surface find homes for themselves. Cleaning tasks prioritize themselves with lightning speed: the drapes don't really need to be dry-cleaned, but the dust bunnies have to come out of the corners. Someone could probably make a good living by charging these folks a fee to visit them on a regular basis just so they'd do their cleaning.

THE HIT-AND-RUN CLEANER

You walk into the bathroom and notice something growing on the shower curtain. You squirt it with cleaner and wipe it off, feeling no obligation whatsoever to clean the equally dirty bathtub, sink, or mirror.

You are a Hit-and-Run Cleaner. Instead of setting aside a specific time for cleaning, you clean as you go through the day, washing or wiping whatever is too large or disgusting for you to ignore. By occupation, you are probably a kindergarten teacher or an emergency medical technician.

THE IMPAIRED CLEANER

For one reason or another, the Impaired Cleaner simply doesn't clean, or not so you'd notice. If he was accused of cleaning, there wouldn't be enough evidence to convict him. The floors in an Impaired Cleaner's house may be hardwood or carpeted, but it's impossible to tell, since you can't see the floors. Clean and dirty dishes look about the same. Clothes, whether clean or dirty, generally live in piles, and it's sometimes hard to tell which is which.

The reasons for this condition lie deep within the Impaired Cleaner's psyche, which probably hasn't been cleaned in ages either.

THE SELECTIVE CLEANER

This is the person who is compulsive about some cleaning tasks and totally ignorant of others. The average male, for example, keeps his car clean enough to perform organ transplants inside but can walk over a pile of laundry the size of Mount St. Helens without even noticing it. Teenage girls can be scrupulous about cleaning their bodies, while their bedrooms look like the scene of a tornado.

Selective Cleaners often have difficulties with relationships, since they also ignore personal problems, such as the fact that their spouse works at a fast-food restaurant but wears Armani suits and drives a Porsche.

THE TRULY COMMITTED CLEANER

This is the type of person for whom cleaning is a kind of sacrament — your Aunt Edna, who vacuums three times a day and makes you take your shoes off before you enter her house, where you're afraid to have an impure thought for fear of dirtying the air. For the Truly Committed Cleaner, cleaning requires a level of commitment akin to taking religious vows, something one is called to. Generally, Truly Committed Cleaners are the first-born children in their families and, like all zealots, drive the rest of us crazy. Those of us who came into the world later tend to have a more relaxed attitude toward cleaning. In fact, we couldn't care less.

ESSENTIAL EQUIPMENT

The average supermarket, hardware store, or department store carries approximately 2,127 different tools designed to help you clean every nook and cranny of your home. We have found, however, that there are only a few basic tools you really need to keep a tidy house. Besides the obvious (broom, dustpan, vacuum cleaner, wet mop, and dry mop), you'll need the following.

Bottles & dispensers   When you run out of a commercial cleaner, save the bottle. Generally, you can replace the cleaner with your own concoction that works just as well and costs a lot less. You can also buy empty pump, squirt, and spray bottles at the hardware store — but why spend the money? Just be sure to clean your bottles thoroughly and label them clearly for safety's sake.

Buckets & basins   You'll need at least a couple of plastic buckets and basins for various cleaning projects. Plastic paint buckets with metal handles are cheap and great for cleaning. Choose different-colored basins for different tasks to make cleaning easier (for example, a blue basin for soaking stained clothing and a brown basin for washing floors or other really dirty jobs).

Paintbrushes   Paintbrushes are useful for a lot more than just painting. The next time you see one of those cheap selections of brushes of various sizes at a flea market or discount store, pick some up and use them for cleaning everything from coffee grinders to piano keys. Plastic-handled brushes are best for any setting where there's water, as wooden brushes can swell, and the metal parts can rust. Label each brush with its intended purpose, using a permanent marker so as not to confuse it with other brushes.

Rags & paper towels   Paper towels are cheap and handy, though you may want to limit their use to emergency cleanups and special applications if you're concerned about the environment. For everyday cleaning and polishing, rags work fine. The best rags are absorbent, nonshiny cloths such as old diapers or terry cloth hand towels that can be washed and reused over and over. Keep a few worn-out athletic socks — even if they have holes in them — for a variety of cleaning tasks.

Sponges   Not all sponges are created equal. Among the most versatile we've found are nylon-backed scrubbing sponges, which are made for various purposes. Choose the least abrasive for washing dishes, saving heavier-duty sponges for tough jobs. We know it's a lot to ask, but be sure to read the label when you buy a new sponge (which should be often). If you use the wrong sponge for a chore, at the very least you'll cause yourself more work, and at worst you could damage the finish on whatever you're cleaning.

Steel wool   Steel wool is more versatile than we often give it credit for being, but be sure to use the right grade for the job. See the sidebar below for some guidelines.

A Crash "Coarse" in Steel Wool

All steel wool is not created equal. Using the wrong grade of steel wool can increase your work or ruin whatever you're cleaning. Here's a brief guide to steel wool grades and their uses.

0000	Finest	Clean windows and delicate tools
000	Extra fine	Polish metals, remove paint drips
00	Fine	Clean screens, remove old finishes
0	Medium fine	Clean grills and rust from tools
1	Medium	Clean linoleum floors and white-sidewall tires
2	Medium coarse	Remove old wax from floors
3	Coarse	Remove old paint
4	Extra coarse	Remove tough dirt and rust

Toothbrushes   Don't ever throw away an old toothbrush. There are dozens of ways to use retired toothbrushes in cleaning, so replace your family's brushes periodically (say, when the bristles begin to look like a bad patch of crabgrass), and keep the old ones readily available for cleaning.

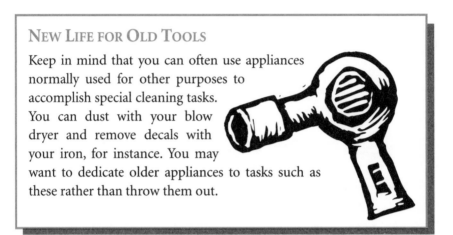

NEW LIFE FOR OLD TOOLS

Keep in mind that you can often use appliances normally used for other purposes to accomplish special cleaning tasks. You can dust with your blow dryer and remove decals with your iron, for instance. You may want to dedicate older appliances to tasks such as these rather than throw them out.

THE CLEANING HALL OF FAME

Over the years, a number of substances have distinguished themselves in meritorious service as cleaning agents. Here are the current members of *The Old Farmer's Almanac* Cleaning Hall of Fame.

Baking soda   That familiar yellow box in the corner of the cabinet or refrigerator has many more uses than simply baking or making the fridge smell better. Baking soda, once called saleratus or nitre, is sodium bicarbonate (or bicarbonate of soda), an alkaline substance used in fire extinguishers, antacids, sparkling water, and innumerable cleaning tips. Baking soda is found naturally in mineral springs or produced from another naturally occurring compound, sodium carbonate (from which we also obtain baking soda's big brother, washing soda or sal soda). As for that familiar muscular trademark, it was borrowed from the Vulcan Spice Mill, which was closed in 1867 when its owner decided to concentrate on marketing baking soda under the trade name Arm & Hammer Saleratus.

Borax   We know borax best as a laundry booster and all-around general-purpose cleaner, but this versatile substance has been around for centuries. According to legend, the ancient Egyptians used it for mummification, and the Romans used it to make glass. Arabian silversmiths used borax in soldering, and Chinese artisans incorporated it into ceramic glazes.

Borax has been mined in the United States, in the Death Valley area of California and Nevada, since the mid-1800s. The famous "20-Mule Team" brand name refers to the transportation method used to haul the substance out of the mines (although the team actually consisted of 18 mules and 2 horses). By 1890, borax was sold for household use as a water softener, detergent, shampoo, facial cleanser, and food preservative.

Today borax is used for many of the same things as in the past (except perhaps embalming). It also is used as an antiseptic, as a corrosion inhibitor in antifreeze, and in the production of glass, fertilizers, and pharmaceuticals.

Cream of tartar   Most of us are familiar with cream of tartar in baking recipes, but it's also useful in a number of cleaning applications. Chemically, cream of tartar is a mild acid, potassium bitartrate. It is the chief ingredient, along with baking soda, in baking powder. The two, when mixed with water, release carbon dioxide, which works as a leavening agent. In times past, cream of tartar was often recommended for whitening clothes and removing rust stains.

Lemon juice   Next to vinegar, lemon juice may be the most versatile substance we've found for cleaning. Lemons were grown as long ago as 4000 B.C. in the Indus Valley of Pakistan, and lemon juice has been used for centuries for cooking, cleaning, and even medicinal purposes. British sailors in the 17th and 18th centuries received a daily ration of lemons to prevent a debilitating (and ultimately fatal) disease called scurvy. The scurvy preventive in lemon juice is ascorbic acid — or, as most of us know it, vitamin C — which is what also makes it a good cleaning agent. With a pH of 2.3, lemon juice is slightly more acidic than vinegar and can often be substituted for it, depending on the application. Vinegar is generally cheaper, but lemon juice smells nicer.

Salt   According to the Salt Institute (there really is one!), there are more than 14,000 uses for salt. In the ancient world, salt was most important as a preservative for food. It was also used as a flavor enhancer, as a medicinal agent, and in many religious rites. Salt was so valuable that it was even used as currency. Roman soldiers received a ration of salt as part of their pay, a practice that led to our word *salary*.

Today we use salt for many of the same purposes as the ancients, as well as myriad commercial applications, such as water softening and the manufacture of soap and glass. In the home, salt acts as a gentle abrasive in cleaning compounds and works wonders for items such as copper and brass.

Vinegar   Vinegar also has been around since ancient times and has been used as a preservative, antiseptic, condiment, and even fire retardant. The Romans covered warships with vinegar-soaked cloths to protect them against flaming missiles.

Basically, vinegar is sour wine or apple cider that has progressed past the point of fermentation. Bacteria act on the alcohol to produce acetic acid, which is what gives vinegar its zing (and makes it a good cleaning agent). The color and flavor of vinegar depend on the alcoholic liquor you start with. According to the Food and Drug Administration, the word *vinegar* by itself means apple cider vinegar.

Throughout this book, whenever we speak of vinegar, we mean white, or distilled, vinegar. White vinegar, sometimes called household vinegar, generally contains about 5 percent acetic acid. You can make a stronger solution of vinegar by simply boiling off some of the water. Of course, the stronger the vinegar, the higher the acid content, and the more carefully the liquid needs to be handled.

HOMEMADE CLEANERS

These days, supermarket shelves contain an arsenal of cleaning products for every imaginable task. However, we've found that you can replace most of these products with a few homemade cleaners that will work just as well and save you money.

Often what you're paying for with commercial products is packaging and marketing: fancy labels, slogans, and jingles. So we've provided those for you. For labels, simply photocopy the recipes, cut them out, and paste them onto the side of a clean squirt or spray bottle. You can purchase these bottles from a grocery or hardware store, or wash out an old one when the commercial product is gone.

In addition to the label, we've also provided a slogan — "It's HomeMade and It's OK!" — and a jingle that you can sing while using the products.

Recipes for our HomeMade cleaners appear throughout the book. Here is a page guide to help you find them quickly.

The HomeMade Cleaner Jingle
(Tune: "I've Been Working on the Railroad")

I've been using HomeMade cleaners
All the live-long day.

I'll be going to Bermuda
With the money that I save.

Can't you hear me always singing
As I sprinkle, spritz, and spray?

I've been using HomeMade cleaners.
"It's HomeMade and It's OK!"

Chapter 2
The Kitchen

I N MOST HOMES, THE KITCHEN IS THE CENTER OF ACTIVITY and therefore in constant need of cleaning. Before we look at specific cleaning chores, here's our number one tip for cleaning in the kitchen (or anywhere else in the house, for that matter): you can generally save yourself a lot of elbow grease by spraying cleaner on and walking away. Most cleaners will loosen dirt and grime all by themselves, saving you from having to scrub, if you just give them some time to work.

DISHES, POTS & PANS

We know it's tempting, but don't let dishes sit too long before you wash them. If you do, the most innocuous substances, such as breakfast cereal, will harden into something strong enough to use as a lining for nuclear reactors. To prevent this, rinse dishes before stacking them and put a little hot water in cups and glasses. You'll save yourself a lot of scrubbing later. If you can, fill the sink or basin with hot, soapy water and let the dishes sit for a few minutes before washing. You'll be amazed at how quickly the gunk slides off.

For extra-greasy dishes, use a grease-cutting dishwashing liquid or add a few drops of ammonia to your dishwater, which also helps cut grease.

Everyone has his or her own approach to washing dishes (see the section on cleaning personalities beginning on page 14), but it makes sense to wash the least soiled items first — glasses and silverware — and work your way up to the really grungy pots and pans.

 With the help of steel wool, now generally procurable, washing the bean pot is no longer a difficult task. (1920)

These days, steel wool is generally considered too harsh for all but the toughest cleaning jobs, having been replaced by plastic net scrubbers, nylon-backed sponges, and an infinite variety of scrub brushes. Nylon-backed sponges come in a variety of strengths, from those that are safe for all dishes to those that can be used only to scrub small meteorites off the heat shield of the space shuttle. We recommend the gentlest type for everyday cleaning.

As a general rule, it's better to rinse dishes in very hot water and let them air-dry. No, we're not just being lazy; air-drying is more sanitary. If you can't stand the sight of a "Leaning Tower of Dishes" and you simply must dry, use terry cloth towels, as they are more absorbent than other towels.

Now on to the specific suggestions.

Baby bottles   You can wash the nipples and caps of baby bottles (as well as the bottles themselves) in your dishwasher. Put the nipples and caps in a small mesh bag (the kind pantyhose are washed in) and tie the bag to the dishwasher's top rack. Run the machine through a complete wash cycle.

Another way to clean baby bottle nipples is to place them in a glass jar of water with a tablespoon of vinegar added. Boil the water in the microwave for a few minutes.

To get rid of sour milk smell in a baby bottle, place a teaspoon of baking soda in the bottle, fill with warm water, and shake to dissolve. Leave overnight, then wash and sterilize.

Canisters (metal)   Metal canisters, such as those used to store flour, sugar, or cookies, can develop rust along the seams if not completely dried after washing. To get rid of all the moisture quickly, aim your hair dryer at them for a minute. (Hey, it works in restaurant restrooms, why not at home?)

What's the Difference Between . . .

Dishwashing liquid and dishwasher detergent? Detergents formulated for dishwashers (whether liquid or powdered) are stronger than liquids designed for hand-washing dishes. Automatic dishwasher detergents can be useful for other cleaning projects besides washing dishes, but they should be used with caution, as they are quite caustic.

Cleaners and *Cleansers?* According to the *American Heritage Dictionary* (3rd edition), a cleaner is "one whose work or business is cleaning" or "a machine or substance used in cleaning." A cleanser is "a detergent, powder, or other chemical agent that removes dirt, grease, or stains." In everyday usage, the terms are often used interchangeably, with some exceptions. Phrases such as "oven cleaner" and "window cleaner" are fairly standard, and powdered cleaning compounds are generally referred to as "cleansers." In this book, we generally use "cleaner," reserving "cleanser" for powders.

China   Use only mild dishwashing liquid to clean your fine china. Avoid harsh abrasives, especially if the china is gilded.

Remove stains from china with a paste of vinegar and salt. Apply the paste and let it sit for a while, then rinse it off. You can also use a paste of baking soda and water or powdered dishwasher detergent and water.

For bad stains, soak the china in a mixture of 1 tablespoon bleach and 1 quart water until the stain is gone.

Coffee cups & teacups   Stains in coffee cups and teacups will clean up nicely if you scrub them with a damp sponge dipped in baking soda. Baking soda paste won't scratch like some abrasive cleansers, which can actually leave more places for stains to settle. If you find you need a bit more scrubbing power, mix a little salt in with the baking soda.

Coolers & picnic jugs   There's nothing quite like opening a picnic jug and smelling the mildewed remains of your last picnic punch. To remove odors from coolers and jugs, scrub the inside with baking soda. For extreme cases of mildew, use a strong solution of vinegar and water. (If you're desperate, you can use a bit of bleach instead, as bleach is strongly antifungal. But for drinking containers, we prefer something a bit less noxious. If you do use bleach, rinse extremely well.)

To prevent musty smells and mildew in the future, make sure the cooler or jug is absolutely dry before you put it away, and leave the cover slightly ajar to allow air to circulate inside.

Crystal   You can use vinegar to wash crystal without leaving spots or streaks. Put 1 cup vinegar in a basin of warm water, wash crystal carefully, and air-dry.

Glasses, glass bottles & decanters   If your glasses tend to have a film and spots on them, put some white vinegar in a dish in your dishwasher and run the glasses through the regular cycle. The slightly acidic vinegar should solve the problem.

 To clean the inside of a water bottle or any glass that is too small to insert the hand into, put in the bottle a small quantity of tea leaves, pour in about one-third of a teacupful of vinegar, shake well, empty, and then rinse with cold water. (1919)

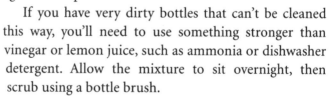

There are dozens of variations on the theme for glass cleaning given above. For lightly soiled bottles, fill them three-quarters full with hot water and add a tablespoon or two of vinegar (more for larger containers). Shake it up and let it sit for a while. Then empty the container, rinse with water, and dry. Lemon juice and water or baking soda and water also may be used, but vinegar seems to work best.

For heavier stains and mineral deposits, let the mixture sit for a time (the heavier the stain, the longer the soak), then add a tablespoon or two of uncooked rice and shake. The rice will act as a scrubber, polishing off the deposits.

If you have very dirty bottles that can't be cleaned this way, you'll need to use something stronger than vinegar or lemon juice, such as ammonia or dishwasher detergent. Allow the mixture to sit overnight, then scrub using a bottle brush.

Occasionally, scratches in glass and mirrors can become stained. To remove such stains, mix a bit of dry mustard with enough vinegar to make a paste. Work the paste into the scratch and rub until the stain is gone, then rinse well.

Griddles   Soaking usually works for regular pancake griddles. For older griddles without a nonstick surface, you can remove burned-on grease and gunk by scrubbing with a pumice stone. (See page 128 for the nitty-gritty on pumice.) This probably isn't a good idea for nonstick surfaces, no matter how tough the manufacturer says they are.

Lunch boxes   Depending on what your child *didn't* eat today, a lunch box can take on a life of its own. Fortunately, modern lunch boxes are mostly plastic (unlike the miniature metal suitcases we carried when we were kids) and can easily be soaked in the sink or washed with our HomeMade General-Purpose Cleaner (page 43). Occasionally, it's a good idea to fill  them with water and a little vinegar or baking soda to discourage germs, then rinse well. If you're really worried about germs (what *was* that he brought home?), add a capful of bleach to the water and rinse well afterward.

 Butter tubs and other vessels which have become foul by use can be easily cleansed by filling them with any kind of meal or bran and water and permitting them to stand till fermentation takes place. Casks which have from any cause become filthy and musty may be cleansed in this way. And inasmuch as this mixture, after having performed this operation, becomes more suitable for swine, there is no expense attending it. (1830)

Muffin pans   Muffin pans can be among the hardest pans to clean. Start by soaking them in hot, soapy water until the crusty remains are soft, then scrub with a vegetable brush. The round shape of the brush will reach into the cups easily.

Plastic containers   You are no doubt familiar with "The Red Badge of Spaghetti." Who hasn't tried to scrub those red stains left on plastic containers by spaghetti sauce or other tomato-based substances? One way to avoid such stains is to spray a light coating of cooking spray inside the container before filling it with sauce. Later, when washing up, rinse the sauce off in cold water first, to prevent stains from setting.

If a stain has already set, try scrubbing it with a paste made of lemon juice and baking soda. Or simply rinse with lemon juice and set the container in the sun for a day to bleach out the stain. You'd be surprised how well this works.

For really stubborn stains, you could try bleaching them out, but we consider this a last resort. Plastics can absorb strong chemicals (that's how you got the stain in the first place), and most folks don't appreciate the subtle bouquet of chlorine in their marinara sauce.

Pots & pans   The easiest way to remove really thick grime from pots and pans is to cover the gunk with hot water and let it soak for a while. For extra-greasy, burned-on food, such as grease from a roast, dampen the area with hot water and sprinkle with baking soda. Cover this with a damp paper towel (to keep it moist while the crud loosens) and let it sit for at least an hour. You should be able to mop the grease right up.

If you're impatient (or in a rush), sprinkle the bottom of the pan with baking soda or powdered dishwasher detergent, add enough water to cover, and boil gently until the burned-on material is loosened.

If all else fails and you have a self-cleaning oven, try cleaning all-metal pots and pans by putting them in the oven when you clean it. By

MAKE A BAKING SODA SHAKER

Make your own dispenser for baking soda by using an empty spice jar (large size) with a shaker top. Or punch holes in the plastic lid of a small powdered-drink can.

morning, any burned-on food in the pans should be a fine powder that can be wiped away.

To remove burned-on food from glass baking dishes, cover the crud with oven cleaner (either a commercial brand or our HomeMade Oven Cleaner on page 41). Let the cleaner sit for 30 minutes, then rinse. Wear rubber gloves and be careful, as most oven cleaners are highly caustic.

BE KIND TO YOUR FRYING PANS

Be especially careful washing frying pans, as overaggressive scouring can ruin them. Nonstick pans can lose their coating, which can end up in your food, travel to your brain, and causes you to run for public office, add on an in-law apartment, or experience other forms of insanity. Similarly, experienced cooks know that you should never scrub cast-iron pans with harsh detergents, as this can ruin the that has built up over time. To clean these pans, soak encrusted foods right away, then scrub using a nylon-backed sponge and plain hot water (or just a little mild dishwashing liquid). To help preserve cast-iron pans, every time you clean the pan, sprinkle a few drops of salad oil on the surface and rub it in before putting the pan away.

To remove the tarlike substance that can burn on the outside of cast-iron pans, put them on the grill of your barbecue after your next cookout, just as the coals are cooling off. The heat will loosen the greasy gunk so that you can remove it without ruining the finish.

Aluminum pans can sometimes get dark stains on them. To remove these stains, mix 1 tablespoon cream of tarter with 1 quart water and boil in the pan. Another trick is to boil 2 tablespoons vinegar and 1 quart water in the pan.

For tips on cleaning copper-bottomed frying pans, see Brass & copper (page 30).

Vases   Most of the tips for cleaning glass containers (see page 26) also
work for vases of all types.

Waffle irons   To remove burned-on batter and
grease from removable waffle iron grids, soak them in
hot water with a few capfuls of ammonia, then scrub
and rinse well. If the grids can't be removed, dampen a
few paper towels with ammonia and close them inside
the waffle iron overnight. By morning, any food or grease
should wash off easily. Rinse well!

METALS

Brass & copper   Homegrown solutions for keeping brass and copper
shiny are in good supply, but you might not have heard this one.

*For polishing brass or copper, make a paste of rottenstone and
cottonseed oil. If there are bad spots or stains, use a little oxalic
acid solution to remove them, but rinse off immediately with
warm water and rub over with the cottonseed oil. (1911)*

Rottenstone? Stones can't rot, can they? Actually, they can. Rottenstone is decomposed limestone, a soft powder that's used for polishing.
You can still find it at some stores that sell or repair furniture. Cottonseed
oil is the yellowish oil that comes from cottonseed. These days, it's used
with other oils to make vegetable oil or shortening. (You could probably
substitute vegetable oil in the tip above.)

Oxalic acid is an organic acid that comes from a number of plants,
such as spinach. It is used in commercial rust removers, which can be
found at hardware stores. (*Note:* This is a caustic substance. Use it
with caution.)

*The water in which common white beans have been boiled will
clean brass. A mixture of salt and vinegar will do the same. (1905)*

Sometimes the old ideas are still the best. We've seen many suggestions for cleaning brass and copper without using commercial polishes,
but this one still beats them all. Cover the surface with vinegar (a spray

bottle makes this easy), then sprinkle with salt. On copper-bottomed pans, you can actually see the tarnish begin to disappear. Scrub with a sponge and rinse away the tarnish. For heavy tarnish and spots, you may have to repeat the process.

Ammonia water will remove verdigris, the green coating that forms on brass andirons or other like metallic articles. (1911)

If you prefer working with a paste, mix equal parts salt and flour with just enough vinegar to make a paste. Apply to the surface, polish, rinse well, and dry.

You can use lemon juice or sour milk instead of vinegar (like vinegar, they are slightly acidic), but we've found they don't work as well. A cut lemon dipped in salt is handy for scrubbing spots on brass or copper.

IT'S A CLEANER! IT'S A SALAD DRESSING!

Put a little olive oil on a clean cloth and rub it on brass items to prevent tarnishing. For brass items not used for cooking (doorknobs, drawer hinges, and the like), you can use paste wax after cleaning to prevent tarnish from returning.

Bronze   Many of the methods for cleaning brass and copper also work for bronze, which is an alloy of copper and other metals.

Cleanse all bronze articles by rubbing with a soft cloth moistened with sweet oil. Polish afterward with an oily chamois. All dust must be removed before attempting to clean and polish. (1922)

Chrome   You won't find references to chrome in the older editions of *The Old Farmer's Almanac,* since the practice of plating metals with chromium to give them a bright, lustrous finish didn't become widespread until the 20th century.

These days, chrome is everywhere, from coffeemakers to faucets and toothbrush holders. And we've run across more ways to clean chrome than just about any other material in the home. You name it, and someone says you can clean chrome with it. Among the odd suggestions are the following:

■ Flour, rubbed over the surface with a soft cloth. This works for light cleaning, sort of, but then you have to clean yourself, since you'll probably have flour all over you.

■ Rubbing alcohol, also applied with a soft cloth. This works OK, but not as well as some of the other methods, and it can leave your kitchen smelling like a doctor's office.

■ Aluminum foil, scrunched up, perhaps with a bit of water. No matter what anyone says, this will scratch the thin metal plating of chrome. Unless you're going for a satin finish, don't do it. Avoid abrasive powdered cleansers on chrome for the same reason.

We've also seen lemon juice, ammonia, and club soda recommended for cleaning chrome. All of these work, but not as well as vinegar or a paste of baking soda and water. For everyday cleaning, vinegar is the easiest substance to use. For stubborn, stuck-on crud, baking soda is the clear winner, but it involves a two-step process: apply the paste, then buff dry.

After cleaning, put just a dab of baby oil on chrome and buff well to give it a nice shine.

Pewter   As anyone knows who has ever dropped it, pewter (an alloy of tin with other metals) is very soft. Ask any jeweler: engraving pewter is like carving butter, and it's easy to cut too deep.

It's also easy to ruin pewter with overaggressive cleaning, so take care, especially with antique pewter, which has a different (and softer) composition than modern pewter.

Pewter has been around since ancient times, and so have ways to clean it, often with archaic ingredients. Take this advice from *Consult Me,* a compendium of helpful hints for homemakers published in 1902: "Scour it with fine calais sand in a solution of potass, or soda, with a little oil of tartar. Dry and polish with whiting."

Despite the antiquated ingredients (who knows what "calais sand" is?), this method follows the classic formula for a pewter cleaner: a slightly alkaline or acidic substance with a mild abrasive to remove tarnish and minor scratches. "Potass" (potash) is essentially lye, which comes from wood ashes (see the sidebar on soap making on pages 68–69). In fact, one time-tested method of cleaning pewter is to make a paste of wood ashes and water. Polish the pewter with the paste, rinse well, and buff with a clean, soft cloth.

Similarly, whiting is a chalklike substance used to make window putty. You can still buy it at hardware stores (look for dry putty). Mix some with a little rubbing alcohol and use the paste to polish your pewter.

Another classic pewter-polishing technique calls for using a paste of rottenstone and olive, vegetable, or boiled linseed oil. If you don't have rottenstone handy, a paste of vinegar, flour, and salt (which acts as an abrasive) also works.

Finally, in the odd advice category, we're told you can polish pewter with cabbage leaves. Journalistic integrity requires (well, it doesn't actually require, but it does suggest very strongly) that we admit we haven't tried this. However, if it does work, it's because cabbage has a fair amount of ascorbic acid in it to act as a cleaner.

Silver   *The Old Farmer's Almanac* provided this recipe for an inexpensive silver polish:

 Dissolve ¼ of a box of pearline in a quart of boiling water, cool, and add 5 pounds of Paris white and 2 ounces of castor oil. The mixture should be athick paste. (1911)

These days, Paris white, castor oil, and pearline might be hard to come by. Instead (or if you run out of regular silver polish), toothpaste (not the gel type) makes a good replacement. An old powder puff works well to apply and buff the polish, and you can use pipe cleaners to polish between the tines of forks.

Another solution appeared in the 1904 edition of the Almanac: "If table silver be washed with hot water and soap with occasionally a little ammonia, it can be kept bright without powder or paste."

If you'd rather avoid using ammonia, try soaking the silverware in sour milk for half an hour, then buff dry.

For really tarnished silver (or if you're feeling lazy), try this. Bring a pan of water to a boil and add 1 to 2 teaspoons salt and 1 to 2 teaspoons baking soda. Place the silver in the water with a piece of aluminum foil and simmer for 2 to 3 minutes. Rinse the silver well, then use a soft cloth (an old powder puff also works well) to buff dry. (*Note:* This technique can actually work *too* well, cleaning the crevices that make the design visible, so use caution. You can use cream of tartar in place of salt and baking soda.)

In the "Get a Life Department," we are told that one can puree banana peels and use the result to polish silver. That may be true, but anyone who can afford a food processor with which to puree bananas doesn't need to save money on silver polish. (Besides, regular silver polish is unlikely to attract fruit flies.)

Stainless steel   Stainless steel is another material for which dozens of cleaning suggestions have been offered, including everything from rubbing alcohol to strong coffee.

For our money, baking soda works best. Make a paste with water, or simply wet the metal and sprinkle baking soda over it. Rub with a clean cloth or sponge, rinse, and buff dry.

If you don't have baking soda handy (and if not, why not?), try club soda, which also works well.

APPLIANCES

Early readers of *The Old Farmer's Almanac* would have been befuddled by the number of gadgets and appliances found in today's kitchen. Here are some tips to help keep your coffeemaker clean and your toaster twinkling.

To clean the outside of most appliances, use our HomeMade General-Purpose Cleaner (page 43) or our HomeMade Glass Cleaner (page 113). Protect the finish of appliances by avoiding abrasive powders, and be sure to dry any parts well before you put them back together, to prevent rust and corrosion.

Blender   To clean your blender or food processor and get all the food bits out from around the blades, simply put hot water in it, add a small amount of dishwashing liquid, and blend for 30 seconds to 1 minute. Rinse well and dry.

Can opener   Keeping your can opener clean, whether hand-operated or electric, will make it work better and last longer. Use an old toothbrush or pipe cleaner dipped in hot, soapy water to clean around the cutting wheel. If you need more cleaning power, dip the brush or pipe cleaner in baking soda before scrubbing.

For a hand-operated opener with stubborn grime (which means you haven't been cleaning it often enough), you can toss the whole thing in hot, soapy dishwater and let it soak for a while before scrubbing. Be sure to dry the opener well to prevent corrosion around the cutting wheel.

Chrome   Many kitchen appliances have chrome surfaces, since it makes them prettier. See page 32 for tips on cleaning chrome. A terry cloth dishtowel is ideal for applying and buffing these surfaces.

Coffee grinder   Those little coffee grinders that many of us are so fond of can get grunged up with pulverized coffee in the crevices and around the cutting blades. Eventually, this can reduce the effectiveness of the grinder (not to mention imparting the taste of hazelnut to all your coffee). Buy yourself a small, soft paintbrush to clean out the powder, or dedicate an old toothbrush to the task.

Coffeemaker & teakettle   Ever wonder why the coffee from some coffee shops tastes great, while the brew from the office coffeepot could be used to clean barnacles off battleships? It's because the smarter shops clean their coffeemakers and coffeepots frequently. Not cleaning the coffeepot results in overly acidic and downright nasty-tasting coffee. (We've had coffee at roadside diners that taste as if the machine hasn't been cleaned since V-J Day.)

There are commercial products that remove the acids and mineral deposits that build up on coffeemakers and teakettles, but you can do the task easily without them. Just add 2 tablespoons vinegar to 1 quart water and run it through the coffeemaker. Then run clean water through the unit at least once (more if you can still smell the vinegar). If it's been a while since you've cleaned your coffeemaker, you may have to use a stronger solution of vinegar — right up to straight vinegar. Just be sure to run clean water through it several times to remove all the vinegar. And save the used vinegar to run through the coffeemaker next time or to use as a drain cleaner (see page 42). There's still a lot of cleaning power in it!

For teakettles, whether glass or metallic, boil the vinegar-water mixture for 10 to 15 minutes to remove accumulated mineral deposits.

You can also clean teapots and stovetop coffeepots by adding 2 to 3 tablespoons baking soda (cream of tartar also works) to a pot of water and boiling it for 10 to 15 minutes. When the water is cool, scrub the inside (if you can reach it) and rinse thoroughly.

Dishwasher   The same vinegar that removes streaks and spots from your dishes can clean the dishwasher as well. To remove stains and mineral deposits caused by hard water, put a cup or two of vinegar in a shallow bowl and set it in the bottom rack of the dishwasher. Run the washer through the wash and rinse cycle, stopping it after it drains (no need to waste the energy on the drying cycle).

Believe it or not, you can also clean your dishwasher (not to mention make it smell nice) by filling the detergent cup with powdered lemonade mix and running it through the regular cycle. The ascorbic acid (that's the fancy name for vitamin C) in the mix cleans in the same way the acetic acid in vinegar does. Again, save energy by stopping the dishwasher before the drying cycle.

Dishing Up a New Invention

Not every tale of invention is a rags-to-riches story.
Here's one that's a riches-to-dishes story.

Josephine Cochrane, a wealthy woman from Shelbyville, Illinois, liked to give large parties. But large parties meant lots of dishes — expensive dishes — many of which ended up broken at the hands of clumsy (or harried) servants.

Cochrane looked around for a mechanical dishwasher that would save time (not to mention dishes). One inventor had patented a hand-cranked dishwasher in 1850, but that wasn't what she had in mind. Frustrated, she decided to build her own. Using stiff wire, a copper boiler, and a motor, she came up with a washer that worked so well her well-to-do neighbors all wanted one as well. Cochrane perfected the design and entered it in the Chicago World's Fair of 1893, where it won the highest award in its category.

Although it took a while for the dishwasher to catch on (at first, only wealthy families and large restaurants and hotels had enough hot water to make it practical), Cochrane founded a company to sell her dishwasher. That company later became KitchenAid, still in business a hundred years later.

Microwave oven   Microwave ovens have their own "self-cleaning" feature. Just put a tablespoon of vinegar or lemon juice (are you getting the idea that these two are often interchangeable?) in a cup of water and boil it in the oven for 2 to 4 minutes (the setting will vary depending on your oven). The idea is to steam up the inside of the oven, which will loosen any burned-on crud. Leave the door closed for a few minutes after steaming, then wipe the oven with a damp cloth.

If you have hardened, burned-on gunk, spray it with our HomeMade General-Purpose Cleaner (page 43). Let it sit for several minutes, then wipe with a damp cloth or sponge. If that doesn't work, try our HomeMade Easy Scrub (page 45).

Mixer   Have you ever tipped the electric mixer back before the beaters stopped spinning and sprayed gobs of cake batter all over the base? Just spritz them with our HomeMade General-Purpose Cleaner (page 43) and let it sit. After a few minutes, the batter should be soft enough to remove without scrubbing.

To clean the many nooks and crannies of an electric mixer, use a cotton swap or toothbrush dipped in warm, soapy water.

Refrigerator   Clean the outside of your refrigerator using our Home-Made General-Purpose Cleaner (page 43). To remove dried-on drips, spray with cleaner and let sit for a few minutes before wiping clean. Letting the cleaner sit prevents your having to scrub with a powdered cleanser, which can eventually dull the surface.

The same technique works for inside the fridge, which you should clean occasionally to prevent it from becoming a laboratory for mildew production. To clean the sides, sprinkle some baking soda on a damp sponge and wipe them down.

Mildew loves the tight spaces between your refrigerator's seals. Make it unwelcome by wiping them down with a sponge dampened with vinegar. If mildew has already colonized, scrub gently with a toothbrush dipped in vinegar. Use vinegar in any other parts of the fridge where mildew has grown.

Don't forget to clean behind and underneath your refrigerator. Refrigerators are basically designed to move heat from inside the unit to outside, and they need freely circulating air to work efficiently. Vacuum behind the fridge, including the coils if they're exposed. Clean under the fridge by placing an old nylon stocking or a long sock over a yardstick and sliding it around underneath.

Icemaker If the ice cubes from your automatic icemaker start to taste funny, it's time to clean that as well. Wash any removable parts (ice cube trays, bin) with baking soda and water, and wipe down the icemaker, too.

Odors If odors are a problem in your refrigerator, place an open box of baking soda in the back to absorb them. A dish of charcoal briquettes also will absorb odors. For better absorption, place the briquettes in a paper bag and pound them with a hammer to break them up into smaller bits. Or use the powdered charcoal designed for potted plants. (Just don't mistake it for dark roast Colombian coffee!)

Vanilla extract doesn't remove odors, but it can provide a pleasant cover-up. Sprinkle a few drops on a sponge and wipe down the inside of the fridge. Or dampen a cotton ball with vanilla and place it in the back. Cinnamon, orange peel, and other spices also can be used as refrigerator potpourri, but be careful: foods in enclosed spaces can absorb odors (even pleasant ones), so wrap them well.

Of course, the other way to prevent odors is to toss out the chili that's been sitting in the back of the fridge for two weeks. Or was it beef stew? When you can't remember, it's time to toss it.

Shelves & racks If the shelves and racks get really dirty, you can wash them in your dishwasher, if they'll fit. When removing shelves, be careful not to break the plastic connectors that hold them in place.

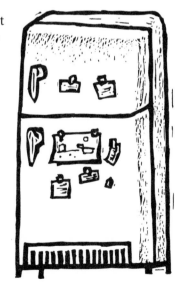

A WASH AND A WAX
If the folks in your house tend to spill a lot, you can make future cleanup easier by wiping the inside of the refrigerator with glycerin or waxing shelves and racks with liquid wax. Future spills will wipe up more easily.

Stove   Use our HomeMade General-Purpose Cleaner (page 43) to clean the outside of your stove. A toothbrush comes in handy for cleaning around knobs and in crevices.

On stovetops, sprinkle spills with salt as they happen. This will make them easier to clean up after the stove has cooled down.

Fan If your stove has a fan with removable parts, it's a good idea to clean them occasionally. Make sure the power to the fan is off before removing the fan cover, filter, and so on. Put a tablespoon or two of ammonia in hot, soapy water (to cut the grease) and soak the removable parts for up to an hour. (The length of soaking time depends on the amount of grease that has accumulated.) Scrub with a soft-bristle brush, rinse well, and dry thoroughly before reassembling.

> ## COLANDER COVER UP
> Frying foods can spatter greasy globs all over your stovetop. To prevent this, take a metal colander that's large enough to cover the pan and turn it upside down over the pan. The colander will trap much of the grease, while allowing heat and steam to escape.

Oven   Self-cleaning ovens are great, but if you don't have one, you're stuck with oven cleaners, which are among the most caustic substances found in the average home. Here are some alternatives, but check your owner's manual before trying any of them on a self-cleaning or continuous-cleaning oven. And always be sure the oven is cool before cleaning it.

For overnight cleaning, put a cup or two of ammonia in a shallow pan and set it on the bottom rack of the oven. The vapors will loosen grease and burned-on food. If you want to increase the grime-loosening power of the ammonia, boil a pan of water and put it beside the ammonia before closing the door. (If you're *very* careful, you can add the ammonia to the boiling water right before putting it in the oven. Just be sure not to inhale the vapors.) In the morning, air out the oven well and proceed with your cleaning.

For lighter spills, simply wiping with a damp sponge or cloth may suffice. For heavier grime, spray on our HomeMade Oven Cleaner (page 41) and let it sit for at least 10 to 20 minutes before removing. (The heavier the gunk, the longer you should let the oven cleaner sit. We usually spray ours on just before going away on vacation.) A small window squeegee makes a handy tool for removing oven cleaner goop.

For extremely tough spills, try using our Home-Made Easy Scrub (page 45) with a piece of fine-grade (000 or 0000) steel wool. Remember, the longer you let a cleaner sit on a spill (as long as it stays moist), the less scrubbing you'll have to do to remove it.

Racks   You can clean oven racks by placing them in the bathtub (protect the bottom with a rubber mat or old towel), sprinkling them with powdered dishwasher detergent (which is stronger than dishwashing liquid), and adding just enough hot water to cover. Let them soak while you clean the rest of the oven, and the grease and grime should come off easily.

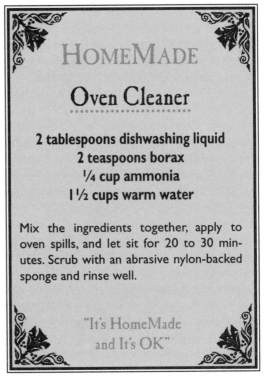

HomeMade
Oven Cleaner

2 tablespoons dishwashing liquid
2 teaspoons borax
¼ cup ammonia
1½ cups warm water

Mix the ingredients together, apply to oven spills, and let sit for 20 to 30 minutes. Scrub with an abrasive nylon-backed sponge and rinse well.

"It's HomeMade
and It's OK"

Another way to clean oven racks is to place them in a heavy garbage bag and spray them with our HomeMade Oven Cleaner (above). Close the bag tightly and let it sit for a few hours or overnight. Then scrub with fine-grade (000 or 0000) steel wool or an abrasive nylon-backed sponge and rinse the cleaner off in the bathtub or outside with a garden hose. You can also do this trick with a commercial oven cleaner, but be sure to follow all safety precautions listed on the product.

Window   If your oven has a window, you can clean it with oven cleaner, but be sure to rinse it well afterward to avoid clouding the glass. For lighter soil, use our HomeMade Glass Cleaner (page 113).

Toaster   Keep a small paintbrush by your toaster to whisk crumbs off the tray and into the trash.

See the section on cleaning chrome (page 32) for tips on cleaning the outside of your toaster.

AROUND THE SINK

To clean the sink, spray the whole area with our HomeMade General-Purpose Cleaner (page 43) or our HomeMade Glass Cleaner (page 113) and let it sit for a few minutes. Then scrub and rinse. A toothbrush is a must for cleaning around the sink, faucets, and drain, where food particles and moisture can combine to deposit grime, mildew, and mineral scale.

Dish drainer   The dish drainer often seems to accumulate grime in its fins and crevices. (Scientists are unsure how this happens, since only clean dishes are generally put into drainers. Maybe there's something to spontaneous generation after all.)

To get rid of drainer scum, fill your sink with enough hot water to cover the bottom of the drainer. Sprinkle baking soda or a nonabrasive powdered cleanser over the bottom and let sit for a few minutes. Scrub with a vegetable brush or toothbrush, rinse, and dry.

Rubber dish mat If the rubber mat under your dish drainer gets soiled and grungy after a while, fill the sink with enough warm water to cover it. Add a squirt of dishwashing liquid and ½ cup bleach as the sink is filling. Soak the mat for 10 to 15 minutes, rinse well, and dry.

Drain   Along with oven cleaners, drain openers are among the most caustic substances in your home. To avoid having to use them, give your drains some periodic maintenance.

The easiest method is simply to pour ½ cup baking soda into the drain and follow with 1 cup very hot or boiling water. For more scrubbing power, add ½ cup salt.

If you like "foaming action," pour 1 cup vinegar into the drain after the baking soda. Wait until the foaming subsides (10 to 20 minutes), then flush with hot water. We're not convinced this actually cleans better, but it may make you *feel* as if you're taking more aggressive action.

Faucets   To shine faucets, just rub them with a piece of lemon peel, rinse, and dry with a soft cloth. Avoid abrasive powdered cleansers, as they can dull the plating or even wear it off over time.

To remove mineral deposits around faucets, apply vinegar (a spray bottle makes this easy), let it sit, and then scrub with a toothbrush.

Garbage disposal   The cleaning tips described under Drain (page 42) also work for garbage disposals.

Another method is to empty a tray of ice cubes and some lemon, orange, or grapefruit rinds into the disposal, then run it as usual.

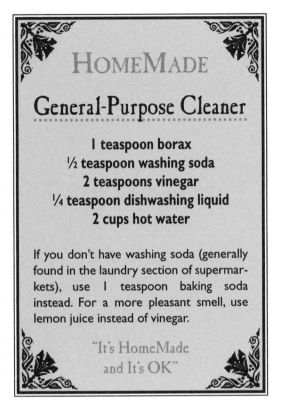

HomeMade

General-Purpose Cleaner

1 teaspoon borax
½ teaspoon washing soda
2 teaspoons vinegar
¼ teaspoon dishwashing liquid
2 cups hot water

If you don't have washing soda (generally found in the laundry section of supermarkets), use 1 teaspoon baking soda instead. For a more pleasant smell, use lemon juice instead of vinegar.

"It's HomeMade and It's OK"

If your dishwasher drains through your garbage disposal, you can give the disposal a quick cleaning by turning it on as the dishwasher is draining. The hot water and detergent from the dishwasher will clean the disposal as well.

Cool It With the Disposal

When using your disposal, run only cold water through it. This seems counterintuitive, since hot water is generally better for cleaning, but hot water also melts grease that can congeal in your pipes and cause hardening of the sink arteries. Cold water simply washes food particles away.

Sponges   Whether natural or man-made, sponges are capable of harboring germs and odors if they are not kept clean.

 Keep sponges clean by washing them now and then in [baking] soda, carefully rinsing out all the soda with pure cold water. (1907)

Besides the baking soda trick above, another way to freshen a sponge is to soak it with lemon juice or vinegar and let it sit for a while. Rinse it well and squeeze dry.

Or place a damp sponge in your microwave oven and heat it for a minute on full power. Any odor-causing bacteria will be fried. (Just be sure to let the sponge cool before you take it out!)

You can also wash sponges in your dishwasher. Use a plastic clothespin or other plastic clip to attach them to the top rack of the dishwasher next time you run it. (You don't want them to fall into the drain and clog it.) The sponges will be cleaned and sterilized by the dishwasher's high heat.

EGG DROP COUP

If you drop an egg while cooking, sprinkle it with salt and let sit for at least 15 minutes. The salt will dry up the egg, which you can simply sweep up later.

SURFACES

Cabinets   Over time, kitchen cabinets collect fingerprints, food spatters, and airborne grease. To remove these, try our HomeMade Heavy-Duty Disinfectant Cleaner (page 51). Spray the cleaner on and let it sit for a few minutes to loosen the dirt and grime, then sponge it off. Rinse out your sponge or cloth and sponge again.

Chrome   See Metals (page 32).

Glass   See Windows (page 111).

Laminated tabletops & countertops   Formica, that laminated plastic material found in just about every kitchen these days, is wonderful stuff, but it's not indestructible. Never clean laminated surfaces with steel wool, harsh abrasive powdered cleansers, or rough scouring pads, as these cleaners can ruin the luster of the surface or even leave scratches. Most spills will wipe off laminated countertops if you do it immediately.

For hardened spills, soak with our HomeMade General-Purpose Cleaner (page 43), let sit for a few minutes, and mop up. If you do need to scrub, use a nonscratching cleanser such as our HomeMade Easy Scrub (at right).

To remove stains from laminated countertops, try one of these methods.

■ Cover the stain with a paste of baking soda and water (or, for more cleaning power, lemon juice). Allow the paste to dry, then scrape it off and rinse the surface.

HOMEMADE

Easy Scrub

³/₄ cup baking soda
¹/₄ cup borax
dishwashing liquid

Combine the baking soda and borax. Mix in enough dishwashing liquid to make a smooth paste. If you prefer a pleasant smell, add ¼ teaspoon lemon juice to the paste.

"It's HomeMade
and It's OK"

■ If blue ink from the labels of meat packages has stained a laminated surface, try using rubbing alcohol to remove it.

■ If you make bread often, you know how flour and gobs of dough get
everywhere. A flat plastic ice scraper (one that won't scratch) makes it easy
to clean up the bigger gobs and keep them from clogging up your sponge
or dishrag.

Marble   Marble may look hard, but it's actually quite porous. If you
spill anything on marble, clean it up immediately, as stains can set quickly.

 Green spots on marble may be removed by applying a paste of
quicklime and washing soda. (1905)

Lime, also known as caustic lime, may be scarce in today's kitchens,
but you may have a lemon handy. Cut a wedge, sprinkle it with salt, and rub
this over marble to clean and remove stains. (Washing soda is a stronger version of baking soda, generally found in the laundry section of supermarkets.)

To polish marble, use silver polish or marble polishing powder (available at hardware stores). You can make your own polish with baking soda,
chalk, or talc mixed with a little water or lemon juice. For tough stains,
apply the paste and cover it with a damp paper towel or cloth (to prevent it
from drying out too quickly). Leave the paste on overnight and dust it off
in the morning.

For really tough stains, you need a stronger solvent. For grease stains,
make a paste of chalk or talc and paint thinner. For ink stains, use alcohol
instead of paint thinner, and for food stains use hydrogen peroxide as the
solvent.

A similar technique for cleaning alabaster surfaces was offered in the
1902 edition of the book *Consult Me:* "If stained, apply fuller's earth, pipe-
clay, or whiting, for three or four hours, then wash off. If very dirty and
stained, first wash with aquafortis [nitric acid] diluted with water." Those
of you who are lucky enough to have alabaster surfaces in your kitchens can
pass this tip along to the servants.

Porcelain cooking surface   To make your porcelain surface last
longer, follow the manufacturer's directions, especially those regarding

cleaning. Wipe up spills immediately, especially if the substance is acidic. Never use abrasive powdered cleansers or scouring pads. If you wipe the surface down with a mild dishwashing liquid and water every time you use it, you probably won't need to do a lot more. If spills do dry on, soak them with water for a few minutes and use a nonscratching powdered cleanser or baking soda.

Stainless steel   Stainless steel stovetops and countertops can be cleaned with club soda.

Surfaces not used for food preparation can be protected and kept sparkling by putting a few drops of lemon oil or baby oil on a soft, clean cloth and rubbing down the surface.

For more tips on cleaning stainless steel, see page 35.

Wooden cutting boards   Wooden cutting boards are notorious for absorbing smells and stains if not properly maintained. To prevent stains, wash your board after each use and wipe it down with mineral oil to season it. (Resist the temptation to use vegetable oil, even though it's probably handy. Vegetable oil can turn rancid and ruin the board.)

To remove odors from a wooden cutting board, rub it with a lemon wedge. Sprinkle the lemon with salt to help remove stains, or rub the stains with a paste of baking soda and water.

If you're concerned about bacteria such as salmonella and E. coli on cutting boards, you need to get more aggressive. Wash the board well in hot, soapy water, then soak for 2 minutes in a solution of 3 tablespoons bleach and 1 gallon water. Rinse well to remove the bleach and dry with a clean cloth. (Note that you shouldn't soak butcher-block cutting boards, as they can absorb water and split or warp. Wipe them down with the bleach mixture, then wipe several times with water and dry well.)

Chapter 3

The Bathroom

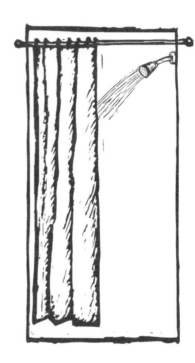

T HE BATHROOM IS PROBABLY THE MOST DISTASTEFUL ROOM IN THE house to clean and the greatest source of cleaning conflict among spouses, families, and roommates. Given the number and variety of bathroom activities — and the fact that everyone in the house uses it — that's probably not surprising.

Here are some ways to keep your bathroom sparkling, which may in turn prevent a few family feuds.

BATHTUB & SHOWER

At last count, there were about 1,127 tub and tile cleaners on the market, most of which contain chemicals strong enough to dissolve gravel. The typical warning label on these cleaners reads, *CAUTION: Contains sodium bi-hydroxy-oreo-sidebyside, which has been shown to cause personality changes in prairie chickens. Avoid contact with polyester. Persons sensitive to highly toxic poisons should wear scuba gear, as inhalation of vapors may impair ability to play the accordion while completing government tax forms.* Most people ignore these warnings, probably because they're printed in type so small you need an electron microscope to read them.

If exotic chemicals bother you, you can make your own tub and tile cleaner (see our HomeMade Heavy-Duty Disinfectant Cleaner on page 51). Or simply sprinkle some baking soda on the area you're cleaning, put a little soap on a wet sponge, and scrub away.

You can also use vinegar as a cleaning agent, but don't mix vinegar and baking soda together unless you want to repeat that seventh-grade science experiment involving a balloon and a soda bottle (an experiment that illustrates the scientific principle that you should never mix vinegar and baking soda together).

And whatever you do, never, ever mix bleach and ammonia or allow them to come into contact with each other (for example, by failing to rinse one away before using the other). Ammonia and bleach react with each other to release chlorine gas, which is extremely poisonous.

Bathtub ring   When it comes to cleaning the bathtub, he who hesitates has a tougher cleaning job. Soap scum can harden on bathtubs, so spray it down with our HomeMade General-Purpose Cleaner (page 43) as soon as you get out of the tub. By the time you've dried off, you can wipe away the scum.

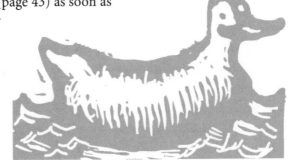

Once the bathtub ring has dried, you may need a stronger cleaner to remove it (see our HomeMade Heavy-Duty Disinfectant Cleaner on page 51). You can also use straight vinegar to cut the scum, or mix some dishwasher detergent in a bucket of water and wash down the tub. (Dishwasher detergent can be hard on your hands, so wear rubber gloves when using this solution.)

For really tough soap scum, pour some rubbing alcohol on your sponge or cloth and scrub with that.

> ### GIVE YOUR BATH THE BRUSH
>
> Use an old toothbrush to clean between tiles, bathtub caulk, faucet handles, and other hard-to-reach spots. Just be sure not to get the cleaning brush mixed up with your current toothbrush.

Decals Those sunflower decals may have looked cute when you stuck them on the tub to prevent slips and falls, but now they're chipped, stained, and ugly. To get rid of them, loosen the glue by soaking the entire decal with vinegar. (Warm the vinegar up in the microwave for a minute to make it work even better.) Let the vinegar sit for a few minutes, then peel off of the decal. You should be able to remove any leftover glue with tub and tile cleaner or our HomeMade Easy Scrub (page 45).

For extremely obstinate decals, you may have to soak them with mineral spirits before attempting to remove them.

Drains Bathroom drains can be an even tougher challenge than those in the kitchen. Without periodic maintenance, the accumulation of soap residue and hair can make bathroom drains sluggish and eventually clog them.

The easiest method for routine cleaning of bathroom drains is to pour

½ cup baking soda, followed by 1 cup vinegar, down the drain. Let these work for 10 to 20 minutes, then flush with plenty of hot or boiling water.

Another method is to use hydrogen peroxide instead of baking soda and vinegar.

If your drain becomes clogged, try using the above methods along with a plunger to force the fluid into the clog. If that doesn't work, you may have to resort to a commercial drain opener. (*Note:* Watch for the word "caustic" on commercial products. The product may burn your skin, and rubber gloves are recommended. Be especially careful not to splash caustic liquids, and never use a plunger with them.)

Try opening the drain with a plumber's snake, or call a plumber.

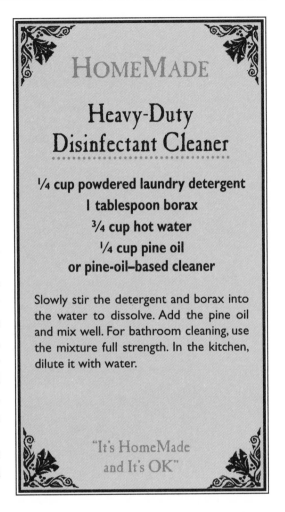

HOMEMADE

Heavy-Duty Disinfectant Cleaner

¼ cup powdered laundry detergent
1 tablespoon borax
¾ cup hot water
¼ cup pine oil
or pine-oil–based cleaner

Slowly stir the detergent and borax into the water to dissolve. Add the pine oil and mix well. For bathroom cleaning, use the mixture full strength. In the kitchen, dilute it with water.

"It's HomeMade and It's OK"

STRAIN YOUR DRAIN

The easiest way to remove gunk from drains is to avoid putting it there in the first place. Use a flat plastic bathtub strainer over the drain to catch hair before it goes through it. You can also use a piece of plastic mesh bag (the kind onions come in) to catch stray hair. Clean the strainer after every bath or shower. If hair gets in the drain anyway, use a cotton swab to reach in and clean it out.

Fiberglass tubs & showers   Cleaning fiberglass tubs and showers requires a bit of caution, since fiberglass scratches easily. Use a paste of baking soda and dishwashing liquid to remove soap film. Vinegar in a spray bottle also works well. Just spray it on and wipe down the sides with water. Whatever you do, avoid abrasive powdered cleansers if at all possible.

You can use a clean sponge mop to wipe down the outside of shower stalls.

After you've cleaned a fiberglass stall, you can put a coat of car wax on the sides to prevent soap buildup and make cleanup easier. For safety's sake, don't wax the floor of a shower unit or tub.

Mats   To clean bathtub mats, spray them down with our Home-Made General-Purpose Cleaner (page 43) or our HomeMade Heavy-Duty Disinfectant Cleaner (page 51) right in the tub. Let the cleaner sit for a few minutes, then scrub and rinse. Lean or stick the mat against the side of the tub to let it drip-dry. It will dry faster and more thoroughly than if left flat on the bottom.

HOMEMADE

Mildew Remover

**1 tablespoon powdered
laundry detergent
1 quart chlorine bleach
2 quarts water**

Combine all the ingredients in a pail. Wearing rubber gloves, wash off the mildew.

"It's HomeMade
and It's OK"

Shower curtains   Like plastic and fiberglass, shower curtains can accumulate soap film and grow mildew. For easy cleaning, keep a spray bottle filled with vinegar in or near the shower and spray them down once or twice a week as you're standing in the shower. The vinegar will cut through soap buildup and deter mildew from growing.

If mildew does build up on shower curtains, it's sometimes easier to clean them in the washing machine. Wash your curtain in warm water and add ½ cup baking soda to

Fun with Fungi

*M*ildew — that disgusting gray, green, black, or red grunge — grows just about anywhere there's constant moisture. It really loves the crevices where bathroom tiles meet and the spaces between the tiles and the tub or shower enclosure.

Technically, the mildew that grows in your bathroom is a fungus, as are mushrooms (isn't *that* a comforting thought?). To find out exactly what kind of fungus grows in bathrooms and how it gets there, we called the customer service number on the back of a commercial bathroom cleaner. A highly trained representative told us that the identity of the fungus in question was proprietary information. (Apparently, even fungi are entitled to privacy when they're in the bathroom. Where are the right-to-know laws when you need them?)

It turns out that fungi spores are everywhere, floating in the air, just waiting to settle on some damp spot and reproduce (another comforting thought for anyone with mycophobia, or fear of fungi). Fortunately, many of the commercial tub and tile cleaners contain a mildewcide, or you can make your own mildew killer by mixing ¼ cup bleach and 1 quart water. Use this mixture to wipe down large areas, or apply it to cracks, crevices, and tile seams using an old toothbrush as a scrubbing tool. (If you don't have an old toothbrush, use your present toothbrush and replace it. It's probably time to change that, too.) Scrubbing with bleach can generally prevent mildew buildup for as long as an hour and a half.

For cleaning large areas of mildew, try our HomeMade Mildew Remover (page 52).

the wash water. If you have a couple of bath towels that need washing, toss them in at the same time. The terry cloth will help clean the curtain.

To prevent mildew from coming back, add 1 cup vinegar to the final rinse water in your washing machine.

Another old-fashioned mildew preventive is to soak the curtain in salt water. This can be done right in the bathtub. Fill it with warm water and pour in ½ cup salt as it fills. Drop the curtain into the tub, soak, and hang it up to drip-dry.

Sometimes mildew will leave a stain if it is not removed promptly. To remove such stains, mix borax with enough vinegar or lemon juice to make a paste and scrub. You can also try bleaching out stains with hydrogen peroxide.

If too much washing leaves your shower curtain stiff and brittle, pour a capful of glycerin or mineral oil into the final rinse water in your washing machine. This will help the curtain (as well as baby pants and other plastic items) stay soft and flexible.

Showerhead   The design of showerheads makes them prone to mineral buildup, especially in hard-water areas. Wiping the showerhead down with vinegar will help prevent such buildup. If minerals accumulate to the point that they are hard to clean or the showerhead becomes clogged, remove the head and soak it in a solution of equal parts hot water and vinegar. For severe buildups, you may have to boil the water gently to dissolve the deposits. You can also use phosphoric acid (available at hardware stores) or a commercial lime remover.

Stains   Porcelain tubs can develop ugly brown stains in areas with hard water. The best stain remover we've found is a paste of cream of tartar and hydrogen peroxide. Make sure it's thick enough to adhere to the sides of your tub. Paint the paste on with an old paintbrush, then cover the paste with damp paper towels to help keep it in place. Leave it on for 30 minutes, then scrub with a bathtub brush or nylon dish scrubber. This method requires very little elbow grease. The only drawback may be the expense of buying enough cream of tartar to cover the tub. A paste of baking soda and peroxide also seems to work, although somewhat less effectively.

SINK & VANITY

Chrome   To clean chrome fixtures in the bathroom, wet them down, sprinkle with baking soda, polish, and buff dry. For more ways to clean chrome, see page 32.

One cleaner you're likely to have handy in the bathroom is toothpaste. If some toothpaste accidentally falls off the toothbrush, don't just wash it down the sink. Rub it on the faucets with your fingers and rinse well for a quick shine. (*Note:* Use only cream toothpaste. The gel type doesn't work.)

Mirrors & windows   Use our HomeMade Glass Cleaner (page 113) to clean bathroom mirrors, windows, and other glass. Try to avoid overspraying the mirror. If the solution drips down and dampens the bottom edge, the moisture can seep between the glass and the silver backing, which will then flake off more easily, especially in sliding-door-type cabinets. Spray the cleaning solution on your sponge or rag instead of directly on the mirror, then rub.

TOILET

Let's face it, cleaning the toilet is probably everyone's least favorite cleaning task. Despite the myriad commercial products that promise to eliminate it, occasionally you still have to take brush in hand and tackle the toilet. And if you find that you're feeling sorry for yourself, just remember how truly unpleasant the job was for your great-grandparents.

 Necessaries [outhouses] often produce a foul atmosphere around them; and as the dwelling is near, the offensive air is often wafted to it, and even when not perceptible, is often operating injuriously. Some prepare these conveniences, and cover with loam or other substances all night soil, so as to do away with all unpleasant and injurious effect. When this is not the case, charcoal, plaster, chloride of lime, or other disinfectants should be thrown into the vault to absorb all noxious odors. (1854)

The old standby for cleaning toilets is borax, the secret ingredient in our HomeMade Toilet Cleaner (page 57) and our HomeMade Easy Scrub

(page 45). For easiest cleaning, squirt the liquid or rub the paste over the inside of the bowl and let it sit for an hour or two. (For extremely dirty or stained toilets, you might want to use a plunger to empty the bowl of water first.) Then scrub with a toilet brush or heavy-duty nylon-backed sponge.

For light cleaning, you can simply sprinkle borax into the bowl and scrub. If you run out of borax, baking soda also will work as a gentle scouring powder.

If you're lazy (like us), sprinkle the borax into the toilet bowl before going to bed. In the morning, stains will be easier to scrub away. You can also use a couple of denture cleaning tablets or vitamin C tablets (the ascorbic acid in them makes an effective cleaner) for overnight cleaning. Simply toss a couple of tablets into the toilet bowl before bed and scrub in the morning.

Another lazy person's trick is to buy an automatic bowl cleaner — one that you can refill. Use it up, then refill it with ordinary laundry bleach and put it back in. The bleach will clean and disinfect automatically each time you flush.

When toilets have been neglected for a long time, hard-water stains and rust can build up, especially under the rim. For extremely tough stains, pour ½ cup bleach into the bowl and let it sit for an hour before scrubbing.

If none of the above methods works, try scrubbing stains with the finest-grade (0000) steel wool dipped in borax or baking soda. We've even used a single-edge razor blade to scrape deposits off a toilet rim, but be very careful not to hurt yourself or the bowl if you do this.

GLOVE RENEWAL

If your rubber cleaning gloves start to get mildewed, turn them inside out and soak them in water with dishwashing liquid. Dry them well before using them again.

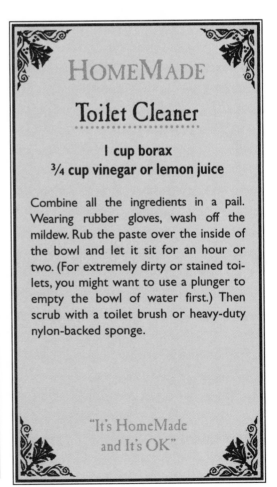

HomeMade

Toilet Cleaner

1 cup borax
¾ cup vinegar or lemon juice

Combine all the ingredients in a pail. Wearing rubber gloves, wash off the mildew. Rub the paste over the inside of the bowl and let it sit for an hour or two. (For extremely dirty or stained toilets, you might want to use a plunger to empty the bowl of water first.) Then scrub with a toilet brush or heavy-duty nylon-backed sponge.

"It's HomeMade
and It's OK"

Chapter 4
Laundry

THE 1854 EDITION OF *THE LADY'S BOOK*, A COLLECTION of wisdom and commentary for women, said, "Our spirits fall with the first rising of steam from the kitchen, and only reach a natural temperature when the clothes are neatly folded in the ironing basket."

Even with modern conveniences, doing laundry still seems like an endless cleaning task. Never is every article of clothing washed, folded, and put away at one time.

We can't do away with washday, but we can pass on some wisdom that you may have missed while Mom was trying to get those grass stains out of your blue jeans or pedal pushers.

EVERYDAY LAUNDERING

Generally speaking, hot water washes clothes better than cold water, so check garment labels and wash in the warmest water recommended for any given item. Detergents also work better in warm or hot water (yes, even "cold-water" detergents), since warmer water facilitates the bonding of detergent to dirt molecules (see "What's Soap, Doc?" on page 68). For fabrics that must be washed in cold water, use a mild liquid laundry detergent, or dissolve powdered detergent in a small amount of warm water before filling the machine with cold water.

Before washing, pretreat heavily soiled areas with a commercial prewash product, or save an empty squirt bottle (the kind dishwashing liquid comes in) and fill it with heavy-duty liquid laundry detergent. This helps you concentrate the detergent on problem areas such as collars and knees.

 A few cents' worth of powdered orrisroot put into [the washing] water will impart a delicate odor to the clothes. This is especially nice for the infant's clothes. (1931)

You may not have any orrisroot (the root of a particularly fragrant iris used in perfumes and cosmetics), but these other laundry additives are readily available.

- Borax is a laundry staple, found in many commercial detergents. Add ½ cup borax to each load to boost your detergent's cleaning power while whitening and deodorizing your clothes.

- One-half cup washing soda (available in the laundry section of supermarkets) also will deodorize clothes.

- To soften clothes and remove any detergent residue, add ½ cup vinegar to the rinse cycle.

- Vinegar also is helpful when washing delicate items. Use 1 to 2 tablespoons in the final rinse to cut through the detergent and reduce the amount of agitation needed to rinse it out.

Following are some suggestions for cleaning a variety of other clothing items.

Afghans   Delicate items such as knitted afghans should be hand-washed in a mild liquid laundry detergent. Here's a little secret we learned from cleaning professionals: a mild dishwashing liquid works as well as more expensive laundry detergents designed for wool and other delicate fabrics. Dry afghans using the air-dry setting on your dryer. For more tips on washing blankets, see Quilts (page 65).

Baby clothes   To clean baby clothes of breast milk, formula, or poop, rinse them immediately, then wash with an enzyme detergent. These substances contain fats, proteins, and other natural ingredients that can make them hard to remove if allowed to sit.

Baseball caps   Baseball caps can lose their shape if you wash them in the washing machine. Instead, wash the cap by hand in cool or lukewarm water using a mild liquid detergent. Find a bowl that's the same size as the cap, turn it over, and shape the cap over it to dry.

Another trick is to do all your baseball caps at once in the top rack of your dishwasher. Use only a little dishwasher detergent, as it is stronger than ordinary laundry detergent.

Berets   Wash berets according to the instructions on the tag. To prevent a beret from losing its shape, stretch it over a plate that's the same size and let it dry.

Curtains & drapes   Here's an easy way to give curtains and drapes a quick cleaning: toss them in the dryer with a fabric softener sheet and tumble on air-dry for a few minutes. This will shake loose dust and freshen them up. For deeper cleaning, some window coverings may be washed at home, but others may need to be dry-cleaned. Check the manufacturer's label for instructions.

Dark pants & skirts   That shine that appears on the seat of well-worn dark-colored pants and skirts can be removed by spritzing with vinegar in a spray bottle.

 A teaspoonful of powdered borax dissolved in a quart of tepid water is good for cleaning black dresses of silk, cashmere, or alpaca. (1876)

Delicates   To wash delicate items in the washing machine, place them in a mesh bag (the kind onions come in) or pillowcase and knot the ends.

Diapers   Washing cloth diapers is a multistep process.

■ First, shake or rinse heavy soil into the toilet.

■ Second, presoak diapers in a pail with a mild detergent and 1 to 2 tablespoons bleach. You can also add ½ cup borax to keep diapers soft.

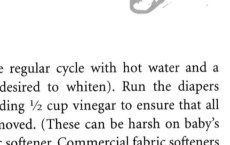

■ Third, when you have enough diapers for a load, put the contents of the pail into the washer. (Don't overload the washer; the diapers need water circulating around them to be thoroughly washed.) Put the washer on the spin cycle to spin off the water (that way you won't have to wring them out).

■ Finally, wash the diapers on the regular cycle with hot water and a mild detergent and bleach (if desired to whiten). Run the diapers through a second rinse cycle, adding ½ cup vinegar to ensure that all the bleach and detergent are removed. (These can be harsh on baby's skin.) Vinegar also acts as a fabric softener. Commercial fabric softeners can make diapers less absorbent — the last thing you want to do!

Electric blankets   Electric blankets can be washed, but you must do so carefully. Set your washer on the gentle cycle and use warm water. Use a mild laundry detergent, and make sure it's dissolved before putting the blanket in the washer. (You may have to let the machine agitate for a minute or two for the powder to dissolve completely.) Set the timer to wash for a few minutes, then rinse. Run the blanket through another rinse cycle to remove any detergent residue. Hang the blanket to dry. Do *not* dry in the dryer, and never dry-clean. Either of these processes can ruin the wiring in the blanket.

Feather pillows   Like electric blankets, feather pillows aren't something you want to wash every week. To freshen them up, toss them in the dryer with a fabric softener sheet and dry on air-dry for 10 to 15 minutes. Before you dry, check for any tears through which feathers might escape, and repair them first.

If pillows need to be washed, fill the washer with warm water and a mild laundry detergent. Wash two pillows at once to balance the load, pressing one into the water on either side of the agitator. Wash on the gentle cycle for a few minutes, stop the washing machine, and turn the pillows over for the remainder of the cycle. Place pillows in the dryer with a couple of tennis balls to help distribute the feathers evenly as they dry. Be prepared for drying to take a long time.

Flannel
To remove stains from flannel is not always easy, but it generally can be done by using equal parts glycerin and yolk of egg. Spread this mixture on the stain, leave for half an hour, and then wash the garment as usual. (1917)

Fur
Dark furs may be cleaned with fine cedar or mahogany sawdust which has been heated in an oven. Alaska sable, seal, electric seal, fox, etc., should be beaten with a switch until free from dust, then laid with the fur side up and the hot sawdust rubbed in. Use plenty of sawdust and don't be afraid to rub. Then place the garment upon a feather pillow with the fur side down, and beat it until all traces of the sawdust have disappeared. After this, hang it in a shady place. (1922)

Handkerchiefs   The following method works for other whites as well.

 To bleach handkerchiefs after washing, let them soak overnight in water in which a bit of cream of tartar has been dissolved. (1905)

Lace
Lace and other delicate items should be hand-washed in lukewarm water with a mild liquid detergent. Avoid bleach or other harsh chemicals, as these can damage the lace. Gently squeeze out the water – don't wring it out – and dry on a flat surface.

You can also make your own mini washing machine for small lace or crocheted items such as doilies. Place the item in a clean jar large enough for it to move around in. Fill the jar three-quarters full of water and add a mild liquid detergent. Shake gently, pour out the soapy water, and rinse with clean water as many times as is necessary to remove all the detergent. Gently squeeze out any excess water and dry flat.

Leather gloves
You can easily wash leather gloves while wearing them. Use lukewarm water and a mild dishwashing liquid or hand soap. Gently scrub any spots with a toothbrush. Rinse thoroughly to remove soap and lay the gloves flat between two towels to dry.

Linens   Over time, white linens can turn yellow from age or the accumulation of body oils (as on pillowcases). The solution is to wash linens frequently, using plenty of detergent. Adding bleach and borax to the wash can help whiten linens.

In times past, folks sometimes boiled linens to get them clean, a practice that seems like too much work today (unless someone in your family is sensitive to the chemicals in commercial detergents and whiteners).

 A little pipe clay in the water used for washing table linen whitens it and saves hard rubbing. A cloth should always be thoroughly rinsed. Plenty of clean water is the secret of clean white linen. (1917)

Pipe clay, as the name implies, is a fine white clay used to make pipes and pottery.

Another way to brighten yellowed linens is to dissolve a couple of denture cleaning tablets in a tub of warm water and soak the linens in it.

See Yellowing (page 79) for more tips.

THE LOWDOWN ON LINT

If lint buildup is a problem on your clothes, add a cup of vinegar to the final rinse. When drying clothes in a machine, throw in a large piece of nylon netting (white netting for white clothes, dark netting for colored clothes) to help remove lint.

You can easily remove lint from corduroy by hanging the fabric while still wet and brushing it with a clothes brush.

To remove lint from velvet, use a sponge powder puff. For other fabrics, use a wet sponge or slightly dampened brush.

Removing lint can be especially tricky when it gets trapped in nooks and crannies (such as the inside corners of men's dress pockets). To remove lint from these places, use a clean mascara brush.

(To clean the brush, soak it in a mixture of 1 cup warm water and 1 tablespoon ammonia, then dry.)

Nylon   To whiten nylon curtains, dissolve some Epsom salts in the wash water.

You can also soak nylon in a solution of baking soda and water to keep it from yellowing.

Oilcloth   In case you were wondering…

 Never use soap on oilcloth. Wash oilcloth with a sponge and cold water and polish with a [piece of] flannel. To improve the color and replenish when dim, beeswax and turpentine mixed and well rubbed in, very sparingly, will be found to greatly improve and restore both the coloring and smoothness of surface. (1918)

Printed fabrics   Printed designs on fabrics, such as the ridiculously expensive T-shirt your daughter brought home from the Defective Armadillos concert, can fade from rubbing against other clothes or hanging in the sun to dry. To make these items last longer, turn them inside out before washing, drying, or hanging them on the line.

Quilts   Grandma's handmade quilt is too delicate to wash in your automatic washer, but that doesn't mean you can't use the machine's tub. Start the cycle and fill the tub with lukewarm water and a mild liquid detergent, then stop the cycle. Place the quilt in the tub and let it sit for several minutes. Advance the machine to the spin cycle to remove the water, then allow the tub to fill with cool water. Spin this out and rinse again until all the soap is gone. (You can also do this in the bathtub, but rinsing takes longer and requires some upper body strength.) Hang the quilt on a line to dry. Machine-drying is too rough for antique quilts.

Rain slickers   If your child's favorite plastic rain slicker is full of smudges, try rubbing them off with a damp cloth dipped in baking soda.

Sleeping bags   To clean a standard sleeping bag (*not* a mega down one), machine-wash in warm water using the gentle cycle. Run through

another cycle without detergent. Dry on low or air-dry, and include a tennis ball in the dryer to help break up lumpiness in the bag.

Sneakers   Remove scuff marks from sneakers by moistening a commercial soap pad and scrubbing.

Whiten white sneakers by washing as usual but adding lemon juice to the final rinse.

When it's time to clean those athletic shoes that cost more than your first house, don't put them in the washer or use any harsh chemicals or abrasives. Start by removing the laces and scrubbing with a mild soap, then rinse. Stuff them with paper towels to help them keep their shape, then drip-dry.

Suede   To remove grease from suede, dip a cloth in vinegar or club soda and use it to sponge the stain. Let dry completely, then use a suede brush to restore the nap.

Sweaters   You can hand-wash sweaters by turning them inside out and placing them in the sink in cool or lukewarm water with a mild liquid detergent. Gently work the suds into the sweater and let sit for 10 minutes. Empty the sink, fill with clean cool water, and repeat until all the soap has been removed. You can also do this in your automatic washer, skipping the agitation and spin cycles.

If you want to soften your sweaters, put some cream rinse (hair conditioner) in the rinse water.

White socks Dirt and grime that's worked into athletic socks can be difficult to remove. To loosen the dirt, soak the socks in washing soda (available in the laundry section of supermarkets) overnight, then launder.

Woolens and wool blankets When it comes to washing wool, not much has changed.

 To avoid shrinkage in washing all-wool goods, dissolve a sufficient quantity of soap in warm water, adding a little sal soda to soften it. Wash, wring, and then rinse in clean warm water, using no cold or very hot water, after which shake well and very quickly. Do not rub on soap or use a washboard. Avoid all patent washing powders or liquids. (1887)

That advice, offered more than a hundred years ago, is still sound. To prevent shrinkage of woolens, avoid washing in very hot or cold water or changing the temperature suddenly. Avoid harsh detergents. And if you're machine-washing an item, use the gentle cycle.

Speaking of detergents, *The Old Farmer's Almanac* offered this method for making your own in 1921, before the advent of liquid detergents: "If woolen blankets are to be washed, it is worthwhile to make a supply of soap solution by cutting the soap into small pieces and boiling the water until dissolved. A good soap free from alkali should be used. A bar of soap makes enough soap solution for two pairs of blankets. The blankets are much softer than if the bar of soap is rubbed over them."

What's Soap, Doc?

If you look around your home, you'll probably find dozens, if not hundreds, of types of soaps and detergents. The two are different, but we'll get to that later.

Soap making originated in ancient times, although no one knows who started it. The process may have come about accidentally as a result of sacrifices in ancient religions. Animal fat from the sacrifices may have fallen on ashes from the wood that was used to burn the offerings, creating the first coarse soap. That process —

cooking animal fat with lye (a strong alkaline substance from wood ashes) – was the basic recipe for making soap for centuries. It wasn't until the 18th century that scientists began to understand why soap results from this process or how it works.

It works like this. Every soap molecule consists of a part that likes water (is hydrophilic) and a part that dislikes water (is hydrophobic). The hydrophobic ends of soap molecules are attracted to dirt particles, surrounding them and exposing their water-friendly parts to the wash water. This makes the dirt soluble in water, allowing it to be rinsed away.

Almost any kind of oil or fat can be used to make soap, from animal fat or grease to coconut, palm, or corn oil. The characteristics of the resulting soap depends on the ingredients used. For example, according to soapologists, soap made from lard (pork fat) cleans well and is quite gentle on your skin, but it lathers poorly. (You don't need lots of bubbles to clean well.) If you want bubbles, you need a vegetable oil base, such as coconut oil (often used to make shaving cream) or olive oil (found in fine castile soap).

Around the turn of the century, scientists developed the first synthetic substitutes for soap, known as detergents. These weren't perfected until World War II, when animal fats (like a lot of other things) became scarce. The good news was that detergents worked in hard water and cold water; true soap does not. The bad news was that, unlike soap, the early detergents couldn't be easily broken down by bacteria and other natural processes. Detergents started building up in cesspools and water supplies, until public concern in the mid-1960s led manufacturers to change their formulas, making detergents biodegradable. (That's why most detergents today say "Contains no phosphates.")

In the early days of our country, most people made their own soap. Store-bought soap was considered a luxury. The 1833 edition of *The American Frugal Housewife* provides a recipe that involves boring small holes in the bottom of a barrel; filling the barrel with wood ashes; pouring water through the ashes to collect a pail of lye (sodium hydroxide, also known as caustic soda); adding three pounds of grease, bacon drippings, lard, or some other form of animal fat; and boiling the mixture until it became thick and ropy.

These days, you'll find a store such as Bath & Body Works or The Body Shop on every corner. These stores offer soaps for every conceivable use and occasion. Soap making at home is still practiced as a hobby by folks who like to experiment with scents, colors, and cleaning characteristics.

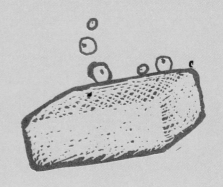

STAINS & SPECIAL CLEANING PROBLEMS

Our foremost piece of advice regarding stain removal is this: do it now. As with many other things in life, stain removal is easier and more effective if you do it right away, before the stain has a chance to set.

 When attempting to remove spots from clothing with benzine or other cleansing material, place an absorbent pad of cloth or blotting paper underneath the spot. Begin the application in a large ring outside the spot and work toward the center. This will prevent the leaving of a dark ring at the edge of the cleaned place. (1920)

These days, benzine is considered too toxic to use as a household cleaner, but the general method for removing spots and stains still holds true. Here are some other general suggestions for stain removal.

■ Scrape or blot away as much of the stain as you can before applying any stain remover. The more you can get off (gently!), the less stain will remain to work into the fabric.

■ Pretest any stain removal product in an inconspicuous spot, especially on expensive or irreplaceable items. We know, this is a pain and takes time, but you'll be glad you did it if you discover that the cleaner you've chosen removes the dye from your expensive designer suit.

■ Turn the stained item over (or inside out) and apply the stain remover from the back side. The idea is to drive the stain out into the cloth or paper towel rather than farther into the fabric.

■ Be sure to leave the stain remover on long enough to give it a chance to work. The more work the remover does, the less you'll have to do.

■ Work from the edges of the stain toward the center, which prevents the stain from spreading outward in a ring.

■ Don't dry or iron the item until the stain is completely gone, or it may set and become impossible to remove.

For tough stains, the 1920 *Old Farmer's Almanac* suggested, "A small scrubbing brush with water alone or with soap and water is an excellent device for removing spots from articles of clothing which are otherwise clean." That indispensable old toothbrush makes a great tool.

Following are some suggestions for removing specific stains.

Berries & juice   Remove as much of the stain as you can by blotting and sponging with cool water. Then stretch the item over a bowl, stain side down, and secure it with rubber bands. (An embroidery hoop also works for this.) Place the bowl in the bathtub or shower and pour boiling water through the stain from a distance of at least three feet. "The force thereby secured is a great help in removing the stain," according to the 1904 *Old Farmer's Almanac.*

For tough stains, try soaking in a solution of one part vinegar and two parts water, then launder as usual. Lemon juice and (for bleach-safe items) hydrogen peroxide have also been suggested for removing juice stains.

Blood   Blot and sponge with cold water. Do not use hot water, which "cooks" the protein in blood and sets the stain. Then try one of the following:

- Cover the stain with a paste of cornstarch and water. Allow it to dry, then brush away.

- Apply a paste of an enzyme detergent and water to the stain to break down the proteins. If you don't have an enzyme detergent handy, apply unflavored meat tenderizer and let it sit for 15 to 30 minutes. Rinse with cool water.

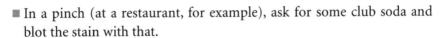

- For fabrics that won't be hurt by ammonia, combine 1 tablespoon ammonia and 1 pint water and soak the stain with the solution. We've also had luck removing bloodstains from white cotton items using hydrogen peroxide.

- In a pinch (at a restaurant, for example), ask for some club soda and blot the stain with that.

Chocolate   Chocolate is another candidate for removal by an enzyme detergent. When that's not available, try soaking the stain in club soda or a mixture of ammonia and water, then washing normally.

Coffee & tea   For fresh coffee or tea stains, try the boiling water trick described under Berries & juice (page 71). For stains that have set, soak the item in a solution of vinegar and water, then hang it in the sun to dry. You may need to use an enzyme detergent to remove tough stains.

Crayon   Minor crayon marks on clothes may come off by scrubbing with a liquid laundry detergent and warm water. For larger marks or melted-on crayon, see Wax (page 78).

Dairy products   Use liquid laundry detergent or a prewash treatment and cool water. (Dairy products contain proteins, which may be set by warm water.)

A solution of 2 tablespoons ammonia and 1 cup water also can remove milk stains.

If the above methods fail to remove the stain, try an enzyme detergent.

Egg   To remove egg from fabric, soak the item in cold water for 30 minutes to 1 hour before washing. Never put an egg-stained item directly in hot water, as this will set the stain.

Grass   Sponge grass stains with alcohol (test on an inconspicuous spot first), then launder as usual.

A solution of 2 tablespoons ammonia and 1 cup water will remove some grass stains.

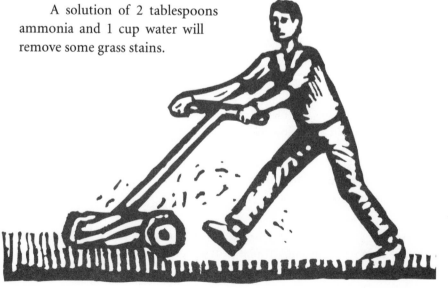

Grease   Remove fresh grease by covering the stain with salt, corn-starch, talcum powder, or powdered laundry detergent. Allow the powder to absorb the grease, then vacuum or gently brush way, repeating until the majority of the grease has been absorbed.

To loosen the remaining grease, rub salad oil or mineral oil into it and wash with detergent and water as hot as the fabric will tolerate. If your water is hard, use distilled water, which is softer and will loosen the grease and work with the detergent better.

Ammonia with salt dissolved in it will remove grease from some fabrics.

For double-knit fabrics, try using club soda.

Gum   The easiest way to remove gum is to freeze it and chip it off. If the item is small enough, put it in a plastic bag and toss it in the freezer. If not, put some ice cubes in a plastic sandwich bag and cover the gum. When the gum is solid, chip and scrape off as much as you can. If any gum remains, soak the spot in vinegar for 10 to 15 minutes, then launder as usual.

Ink   Spanning the centuries, here are several recommendations for removing ink stains.

 To remove ink stains from white cotton, put some cream of tartar on each spot and tie it up with a thread. Put it in a saucepan of cold water over the fire and let it boil. (1871)

Later, in 1907, the Almanac advised removing ink stains with vinegar, lemon juice, or wood sorrel (a cloverlike plant also known as oxalis, from which comes oxalic acid; see page 30).

The classic modern solution is to spritz hair spray on an ink stain, placing a cloth or paper towel under the stain to absorb the ink. Other solvents, such as alcohol or nail polish remover, also may be used.

Lacking those, try rubbing an ink stain with salt and soaking it overnight in milk. This will probably be less effective than the other suggestions.

Lipstick & other makeup   Like other greasy substances, lipstick and other makeup can be removed by using an oily substance, such as vegetable oil, shortening, or petroleum jelly. Cover the stain and let it sit for 5 to 10 minutes. Wash in warm water and laundry detergent to remove the oil. Make sure to remove all the oil, or you'll have a different stain to deal with!

Hair spray also works as a solvent to remove lipstick and makeup stains. Spray it on, let it sit for a minute, and blot away the stain. If you don't have hair spray, try alcohol, nail polish remover, or even cold cream.

Mildew   Mildew is a fungus that thrives in damp places (see page 53), so the first step in removing it is to dry the item in a warm, dry spot. Brush off as much of the mildew as possible, then use a cleaner with an acidic, antifungal component, such as one of the following:

■ A mixture of salt, vinegar, and water (up to full-strength vinegar, depending on the amount of mildew) will work on most fabrics.

■ Remove mildew stains from white fabrics by rubbing with a mixture of lemon juice and salt, then place the item in the sun.

■ To remove mildew from leather bags or shoes, wipe them down with a mixture of equal parts denatured alcohol and water. Allow the leather to air-dry.

■ For very bad mildew infestations, you may need a disinfectant cleaner, such as our HomeMade Heavy-Duty Disinfectant Cleaner (page 51) or our HomeMade Mildew Remover (page 52).

■ Finally, here are a couple of old-fashioned mildew solutions. Soak mildewed items in a strong tea made from thyme, or soak them overnight in buttermilk, then wash. Given the cost of thyme and the smell of buttermilk, you might want to try the other methods first.

Oil   To remove oil stains, make a paste of sugar and water and rub it into the stain. Let it dry, then launder as usual.

You can also rub white chalk into oil stains. Let sit for 10 to 15 minutes, then wash as usual.

Paint   In the past, turpentine or a combination of turpentine and ammonia effectively removed paint from fabric, but it also left a greasy film and a strong smell. These days, better, safer solvents are available. Check the paint can to find the appropriate thinner for the paint you're using, then use this on a clean cloth or sponge to blot up any spills on clothing. (Test on an inconspicuous spot first.)

Here's some old advice that works no matter what solvent you're using.

 If the paint spot is surrounded with cornstarch, it will prevent the turpentine from spreading. (1904)

For water-based paint, blot the area with a solution of warm water and laundry detergent until all the paint is gone.

To remove old, hardened paint, cover the stain with a water-based paint remover (test on an inconspicuous spot first) and let sit until the paint is soft. Scrape away the softened paint and rinse with warm water. If any paint remains, cover it with glycerin and let sit overnight, then rinse clean.

Pencil marks   Pencil marks on fabric can often be removed with an ordinary eraser before washing.

Perspiration   Perspiration stains are often caused by undissolved deodorant. This problem is worse if you have hard water, and installing a water softener might help reduce the frequency of such stains.

For fresh perspiration stains, sponge on a mixture of equal parts ammonia and water, then rinse with clear water.

For older stains, apply straight vinegar (a spray bottle is great for this), let sit, rinse, and launder as usual. Depending on the stain, lemon juice also might work.

Another solution for older stains is to sponge the fabric with a mixture of ¼ cup salt and 1 quart water until the stain disappears.

For more scrubbing power, make a thick paste of baking soda and water, rub it into the stain, let sit for 1 hour, and then launder.

 When soaps are brought into contact with soiled clothing, or with the impurities of the skin, which consist largely of oily matters derived from the exhalations of the body, the alkali in the soap seizes hold of these oily matters and dissolves them, so that they are readily removed by the water. Water alone will not always have this effect, because it has no affinity for oily matters. (1876)

Restaurant mishaps   If you spill something on yourself in a restaurant, ask the waiter for a glass of club soda. Dip your napkin in the soda and blot the stain. Club soda can remove blood, chocolate, coffee, tea, and a variety of other stains – or at least prevent them from drying and setting until you get home to take more aggressive measures.

Ring around the collar   If ring around the collar is a problem, try rubbing shampoo into the collar before washing. Shampoo, formulated to remove grease and oil from hair, works on collars, too. It's also a good way to use up samples of shampoos you don't like.

You also can rub white chalk into dirty collars and let sit overnight before washing.

Rust   Rust stains can appear suddenly on clothing when iron particles in the wash water react with chlorine bleach. If this is a problem in your area, avoid using chlorine bleach or try one of the following methods to remove rust stains.

■ Apply a paste of salt and lemon juice to the stain. Let sit for a few minutes, then pour boiling water through the fabric as described under Berries & juice (page 71). Finally, place the item in the sun to dry.

■ Another old-fashioned rust remover is cream of tartar. Cover the stain with cream of tartar and tie up the ends like a hobo's sack. Dip the pouch in hot water for 5 to 10 minutes, then launder as usual.

If neither of these methods works, you may need to resort to a commercial rust remover. These can be quite toxic, however, so follow the instructions carefully and test on an inconspicuous spot before using.

Scorch marks   Technically, scorch marks are burns, not stains, and removing them may be impossible. Depending on the fabric, however, you may be able to bleach scorch marks out by dampening them and setting the fabric in the sun to dry. Or try applying hydrogen peroxide to the marks and rinse well.

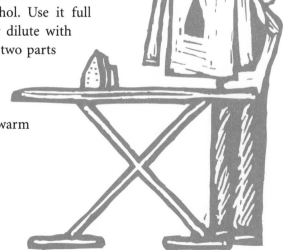

Shoe polish   Shoe polish on fabric is best removed with rubbing alcohol. Use it full strength on white fabrics or dilute with water (one part alcohol and two parts water) for colored fabrics.

Depending on the polish, a mixture of 1 tablespoon ammonia and 1 cup warm water may remove the stain.

Smoke   To remove smoke odors from clothes, hang them above a steaming bathtub filled with hot water and 1 cup vinegar.

Soot   Soot on clothes can often be removed with an art gum eraser.

Or sprinkle the soot with salt, let sit, and then brush off.

Tar   To remove tar from clothing, scrape away as much of the tar as possible, then rub shortening or vegetable oil into it. Blot up the oil and tar mixture and launder as usual.

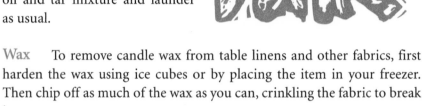

Wax   To remove candle wax from table linens and other fabrics, first harden the wax using ice cubes or by placing the item in your freezer. Then chip off as much of the wax as you can, crinkling the fabric to break it up.

Next, place the fabric between pieces of blotting paper or thick paper towels, stain side down, and apply a warm iron. Move the paper frequently to absorb the wax as it melts out of the fabric.

When you've removed as much of the wax as possible, work vegetable oil into any remaining stain. Allow the oil to sit for 10 to 15 minutes, blot the fabric with a paper towel, and launder as usual, using the hottest water allowable for the fabric. Dry-cleaning fluid may be required to remove some wax stains.

For tips on removing wax from carpets, see page 89.

Wine   Red wine, of course, stains worse than white wine, although both require immediate attention. Blot up as much of the wine as you can, then rinse with cool water or club soda. Apply salt, and if the fabric will stand it, pour boiling water through the stain as described under Berries & juice (page 71). For delicate fabrics, let the salt sit for a few minutes and then rinse in cold water.

For tough stains, try blotting with one of the following: ⅓ cup vinegar mixed with ⅔ cup water; or, two tablespoons ammonia mixed with 1 cup water; or, alcohol, either straight or mixed with an equal amount of water. Rinse well and then launder as usual. In some cases, you may have to use an enzyme detergent to remove wine stains.

 Claret stains may be removed by covering the stain while wet with salt, and after allowing it to stand a few minutes, rinsing it in cold water. (1904)

Yellowing   Some fabrics turn yellow with age or from improper (or insufficient) laundering. Modern detergents often have optical brighteners that can turn yellow if exposed to too much sunlight. We've tried many methods to return white fabrics to pristine whiteness, but none of them works very well. The best approach is prevention: Wash clothes frequently, especially if they come into contact with body oils (pillowcases and collars, for example). Use plenty of detergent and the warmest water allowed for the fabric. If possible, hang to dry in the sun, as sunlight whitens clothes.

Once clothes have turned yellow, you might try one of these solutions.

■ Add ½ cup borax to each wash load.

■ Soak the items in lemon juice and then hang them in the sun to dry.

■ Soak the items in a tub with the strongest detergent you can find, such as dishwasher detergent.

■ As a last resort, you can try bleaching with chlorine bleach. Mix 2 to 4 tablespoons bleach in 1 gallon water and soak for 15 to 30 minutes. Note that bleach can ruin some fabrics, so check the garment label and do this only as a last resort.

LAUNDRY APPLIANCES

Clothespins   Wooden clothespins can turn dark and mildewed when left outside on the line. To prevent them from marking or staining clothes, soak the pins in a mixture of ½ cup bleach and 1 gallon warm water, then rinse in warm water and let dry thoroughly before reusing.

Dryer   Get in the habit of cleaning the lint filter every time you put a load into the dryer. This takes only a few seconds and will increase the efficiency of your dryer. Hang a stiff-bristle brush (such as a baby bottle brush) near the dryer. After you toss in the clothes, pull out the filter and pass the brush over it. Keep a trash bag or basket nearby to collect the lint.

Occasionally (at least once a year), pull the dryer away from the wall and vacuum behind it.

Iron   To keep your steam iron from building up mineral deposits that can clog it and leave spots on your clothes, use only distilled water in it. After the iron cools, pour out any remaining water.

You can remove built-up mineral deposits from your iron by filling it with a solution of equal parts vinegar and water. Allow it to steam for a few minutes, let the iron cool, and rinse with clear water.

To remove cooked-on spray starch from the bottom of your iron, let the iron cool, then wipe down with rubbing alcohol. Be sure to let the alcohol evaporate completely before using the iron again. Or use a paste of baking soda and water to clean the bottom of the iron. Rinse well and dry before reusing.

Washing machine   If your washing machine has a removable filter, clean it by using an old toothbrush to remove any lint. Then soak the filter in vinegar overnight and rinse it with water.

Soap, mineral deposits, and wet lint can build up inside your washer, reducing its efficiency or even causing it to malfunction. Clean the machine once a year by filling it with hot water, adding 1 quart vinegar (or more, depending on how dirty the machine is), and running the machine through its normal wash and rinse cycle.

Lightening Our Load (of Laundry)

For millennia, people scrubbed clothes by hand, rubbing them against rocks beside a stream or in a tub. Later, a high-tech invention called the washboard made life a little easier, but homemakers still had to lug water, heat it on a wood stove, and scrub the clothes by hand using harsh soaps.

To ease the burden, entrepreneurial inventors and frustrated homemakers came up with thousands of devices to make washday easier. As early as 1797, a man named Nathaniel Briggs of New Hampshire received one of the first U.S. patents for his "improvement in washing cloaths." But it was a Philadelphia inventor named Hamilton E. Smith who is generally credited with inventing the mechanical washing machine. Smith's device, patented in 1858, consisted of a wooden tub with paddles and a crank, moving the clothes through the water.

Following Smith's principle, inventors tried hundreds, if not thousands, of variations on the tub-and-paddles idea, sometimes using gas or steam to heat the water or turn the clothes. A few even tried attaching electric motors to the crank, occasionally with shocking results.

The first inventor to perfect the self-contained electric washing machine was a Chicagoan named Alva J. Fisher. Fisher's Thor washer combined a large wooden tub, a series of gears, and a wringer attachment on one side. One thing the Thor didn't have was an on/off switch or safety release, which meant users had to yank the cord quickly if anything other than clothes (such as hair or fingers) got caught in the wringer.

Fisher's patent barely beat out that of F. L. Maytag, a manufacturer of farm implements who had been looking for something to sell in the off-season. In 1907, Maytag introduced the hand-cranked Maytag Pastime washer. He added an electric motor to the washer in 1911, and the new electric model quickly became his company's top-selling product, inspiring Maytag to abandon farm implements in favor of home appliances.

Chapter 5

Floors

ALWAYS UNDERFOOT, THE CARPETS, FLOOR PLANKS, AND linoleum in your house take a beating, getting dirty early and often. Since there are so many different kinds of surfaces, just how you'll clean your floors depends on what the dirt is, what it's on, and how long it's been there. Always know what the manufacturer of your carpet, tile, or other floor covering says before undertaking your cleaning task.

CARPETS & RUGS

 Woolen carpets should be taken up at least once a year, and the dust well beaten out. If kept down longer, the dirt which gets under them and between the threads will wear them out very fast; besides the health of the family requires carpets to be cleaned often. (1904)

Vacuum cleaners may have eliminated the need to beat carpets, but frequent cleaning is still good advice. Walking on dirt in rugs and carpets is like sandpapering them. The grit wears down the fibers, especially in high-traffic areas, making your rugs old before their time.

Clean stains and spills right away. Leaving them gives them a chance to set and makes them harder to remove.

Occasionally, it's a good idea to have your rugs and carpets professionally cleaned, or rent a cleaner from the local hardware store and do it yourself. Even the best regular maintenance can't remove dirt and grime that gets ground deeply into rugs.

STAIN REMOVAL

The rules for removing stains from carpets are similar to those for stains on fabrics (see page 70), especially the first rule.

- Do it now. A little attention to a spill when it happens can save a lot of work (not to mention the carpet) later on.

- Wick up as much of the spill as you can using the corner of a clean white cloth or paper towel.

- Place the cloth over the spill and gently blot up as much as you can.

- Use clean cloths or towels to sponge on whatever cleaning solution you use. Don't scrub, as this can ruin the nap of the rug.

- Clean from the edge of the stain toward the center to avoid spreading the stain.

- Rinse thoroughly to remove the cleaner, or it will become a dirt magnet, and the carpet will quickly become soiled again. A spray bottle is perfect for dampening the area without flooding it and spreading the stain.

■ When the stain is gone, blot up all the liquid by placing a thick layer of paper towels and some heavy books on the area. Change the towels as they become damp, repeating until all the moisture is gone.

In an emergency, you can use club soda to remove stains, or work a bit of shaving cream (which is essentially a very foamy soap) into the stain. Be sure to rinse completely.

Following are some suggestions for removing specific stains.

Blood   Always use cold water (or even ice cubes) to dampen blood-stains, as warm water will set them. After blotting, sponge the stain with a mixture of 2 tablespoons ammonia and 1 cup cold water. Keep sponging and blotting until the stain is completely gone. If that doesn't work, try our HomeMade Rug Cleaner (page 85). If the stain is still visible, try dry-cleaning fluid or call a professional.

Another old-fashioned solution is to cover the stain with salt, then blot with cold water.

Butter   Sprinkle cornmeal on butter stains to absorb the grease, then sponge on our HomeMade Rug Cleaner (page 85).

Candles   See Wax (page 89).

Chocolate   A fresh chocolate stain can be taken up immediately by flushing the area with our HomeMade Rug Cleaner (page 85) and blotting with lots of clean towels, working from the outside in. The key is using a lot of water.

Other chocolate removers include a solution of one part vinegar and two parts water or a solution of 2 tablespoons ammonia and 1 cup water. Both require lots of blotting with clean cloths.

Note that the Carpet and Rug Council recommends dry-cleaning fluid for chocolate stains.

Coffee   If your rug was treated with a stain repellent, cleaning up new coffee spills is easy with cool water and paper towels, or use a solution of one part vinegar and two parts water. An older coffee stain can be treated with our HomeMade Rug Cleaner (page 85) or a commercial spot remover.

Cola   Blot up cola spills immediately and clean with our HomeMade Rug Cleaner (at right). If that doesn't do the trick, try a solution of one part vinegar and two parts water or a solution of 2 tablespoons ammonia and 1 cup water.

To prevent stains, switch to one of the clear soft drinks (which may be sticky but won't show).

Cough medicine   Our HomeMade Rug Cleaner (at right) should remove most of the stain from spilled cough syrup. If a pink tinge remains, try a solution of one part vinegar and two parts water or a solution of 2 tablespoons ammonia and 1 cup water. For a really stubborn stain, you may need a commercial spot remover.

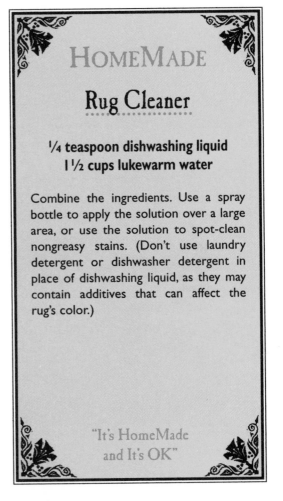

HOMEMADE

Rug Cleaner

¼ teaspoon dishwashing liquid
1½ cups lukewarm water

Combine the ingredients. Use a spray bottle to apply the solution over a large area, or use the solution to spot-clean nongreasy stains. (Don't use laundry detergent or dishwasher detergent in place of dishwashing liquid, as they may contain additives that can affect the rug's color.)

"It's HomeMade and It's OK"

Crayon   The best bet for removing crayon marks (after removing any solid pieces) is dry-cleaning fluid, although our HomeMade Rug Cleaner (above) may work as well.

To remove melted-on crayon, solidify the wax by covering it with a plastic sandwich bag filled with ice cubes, then crunching up and chipping away the wax. Use dry-cleaning fluid or our HomeMade Rug Cleaner (above) to remove any remaining stain.

If you're really brave, you can try covering the melted crayon with a piece of blotting paper and passing a warm iron over it. The crayon willmelt and be absorbed by the paper. Move the paper occasionally to keep the crayon in contact with a clean surface.

Glue   White glue (the kind used in school projects) can be removed from carpets with a sponge and plain warm water. Moisten the area before the glue dries, then blot with a paper towel. Repeat until all the glue is gone. For stubborn spots, mix a bit of vinegar with the water.

To remove old, dried glue from carpeting or upholstery, cover it with warm vinegar and let sit for 10 to 15 minutes. Scrape away the softened glue and repeat if necessary. (Test this on an inconspicuous spot first to make sure the fabric is colorfast.)

Gravy   Gravy stains are generally greasy, so cover them with an absorbent material such as salt or cornstarch to remove as much grease as possible before attempting stain removal. Then use dry-cleaning fluid to

remove the stain. If that doesn't work, try using a solution of 1 teaspoon enzyme detergent and 1 cup water. A solution of 2 tablespoons ammonia and 1 cup water and a solution of one part vinegar and two parts water also have been recommended for some gravy stains.

Grease   Sprinkle grease stains with cornmeal and let it sit until the meal has absorbed as much grease as possible, then vacuum. If any grease remains, repeat the procedure. Follow with our HomeMade Rug Cleaner (page 85). For tough stains, you may have to use dry-cleaning fluid.

Gum   Gum that's stuck to carpets needs to be frozen first. Put some ice cubes in a plastic sandwich bag and cover the gum with the bag. If necessary, break up the frozen gum (pliers work well for this). Scrape it off with a dull knife, then vacuum.

Ink   These days, few of us have bottled ink around the house, or even fountain pens to leak and ruin clothes and carpets. But if you do get an ink spill on the rug, blot up as much as you can, then spray the remainder with hair spray. Blot dry and rinse with a mixture of equal parts vinegar and water. If the stain remains, try a laundry prewash treatment or our HomeMade Rug Cleaner (page 85).

Another trick is to cover the ink spill with salt. Let it sit until the ink is absorbed, then vacuum it up. Repeat until no more ink is absorbed, then use a laundry prewash treatment or our HomeMade Rug Cleaner (page 85).

For stray marks from pens, markers, and stamps, spray on a little hair spray. Let sit for a few minutes, then blot. Repeat until the stain is gone.

Ketchup   To clean ketchup spills, use our HomeMade Rug Cleaner (page 85). If that fails, try sponging with a mixture of 2 tablespoons ammonia and 1 cup water. After that, try a solution of 1 cup vinegar and 2 cups water.

KID-PROOF CARPETING

You will save yourself a lot of carpet cleaning by placing a vinyl tablecloth (the kind with a fabric backing to prevent slippage) beneath your child's chair or highchair. Vinyl is much easier to clean than carpeting.

Lipstick & other makeup   Hair spray works to remove these greasy items. Spray a little on and blot it up. For more on lipstick and other makeup, see page 74.

Mildew   Kill mildew in a rug with a mixture of equal parts vinegar and water. Be sure to dry well, as dampness will only encourage more mildew. If necessary, use a hair dryer on low to dry the carpet.

Mud   Fresh mud will clean up more easily if you sprinkle it with salt, let it dry, and then vacuum it up.

Pet accidents   If your pet has an accident on the rug, it's important to clean up the mess immediately and remove all traces of it so that your pet doesn't get the idea it's OK to relieve himself there again.

Scrape up solids and blot up liquids, then wash with our HomeMade Rug Cleaner (page 85). Rinse with a mixture of ¼ cup vinegar and 1 cup water. If any smell remains, sprinkle with baking soda, let dry, and vacuum.

You can also use club soda or a mixture of 2 teaspoons ammonia and 2 cups water to clean up pet accidents. Again, rinse thoroughly to remove any sign of the mess.

For more on pet problems, see page 132.

Rust   To remove rust stains from carpets, use a commercial rust remover or make a weak solution of oxalic acid (if you can find it at your local hardware store) and water and apply it to the stain. (Wear gloves and use caution, as rust remover and oxalic acid are strong substances.) Let sit, then rinse and blot dry.

Shoe polish   Use hair spray to remove shoe polish. Spray a little on and blot it up. For more on shoe polish, see page 77.

Soot   Sprinkle salt over the soot and gently brush it in to loosen. Vacuum up the salt, then sponge the area with our HomeMade Rug Cleaner (page 85) and rinse well.

Tar   Removing tar from a rug may require dry-cleaning fluid, but you could also try this. Work a small amount of vegetable oil into the tar with your fingers, then blot up the oil. Repeat as necessary to remove most of the tar. Wash with our HomeMade Rug Cleaner (page 85) to remove the oil.

Vomit   Clean up vomit quickly, as stomach acids are strong and can bleach out a carpet's color.

Scrape up solids and blot up liquids. Then rinse with water and blot to remove the gastric juices. Sponge with our HomeMade Rug Cleaner (page 85) or a solution of 1 teaspoon enzyme detergent and 1 cup water.

Wax   Wax will come off a carpet more easily if you freeze it first. Put some ice cubes in a plastic sandwich bag and place the bag on the wax for 10 to 15 minutes. Then chip off the wax, breaking it up if necessary (pliers work well for this). If more wax remains, put blotting paper or absorbent paper towels over the spot and pass a warm iron over it. Keep moving the blotter and iron to absorb the wax. Depending on the color of the wax and the size of the stain, you may have to use dry-cleaning fluid to remove any final traces.

A friend of ours who had a major candle meltdown from the fireplace mantel to the floor and carpet below used a citrus-based cleaner to remove the wax she couldn't chip, peel, or scrape away.

Wine   Blot up wine stains immediately, then sponge with cold water and blot with a clean cloth or paper towels. Keep sponging and blotting until the entire stain is removed. Then sprinkle with salt, let dry, and vacuum. Finally, clean the area with one of the following:

■ One-third cup vinegar and ⅔ cup water

■ Two tablespoons ammonia and 1 cup water

■ Alcohol, either straight or mixed with an equal amount of water

BARE FLOORS

CERAMIC FLOORS

If you're lucky enough to have ceramic tile floors, you probably already know they don't need much cleaning. The grout between the tiles is another matter. For tips on how to clean grout, see Chapter 3.

HARDWOOD FLOORS

Wood floors should be swept and dusted as frequently as possible. As stated earlier, walking over sand, dirt, and dust on your wood floors is like sandpapering them.

After sweeping to remove most of the dirt, dust the floors by wiping them down with a cloth dampened (not soaked) with water. A mop with a removable terry cloth pad or a swivel head works well for this. You can also use a dampened towel wrapped around the head of a broom.

Clean the floor using a mild cleaning product designed for wood floors and as little water as possible.

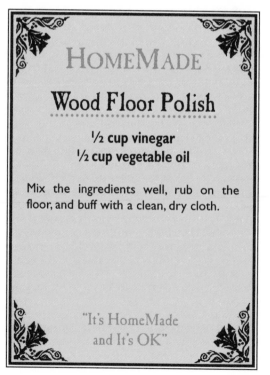

HOMEMADE

Wood Floor Polish

½ cup vinegar
½ cup vegetable oil

Mix the ingredients well, rub on the floor, and buff with a clean, dry cloth.

"It's HomeMade and It's OK"

You can wax wood floors after cleaning, but manufacturers generally don't recommend this. Wax is considered a high-maintenance finish that requires buffing with a polishing machine and, eventually, stripping to remove old wax. Nor are manufacturers big on polish or wood conditioners for wood floors. They simply suggest keeping the floor free of dust and dirt and cleaning it with a mild cleaning product three or four times a year. If you do want to apply a polish to your wood floors, try our HomeMade Wood Floor Polish (at left).

VINYL AND LINOLEUM FLOORS

Like wood floors, vinyl and older linoleum floors should be swept often to prevent scratches and make the finish last longer.

For light cleaning of such floors, plain warm water may suffice, since it will not remove the wax. Use two buckets, one to wash with and another to rinse with, so that you don't put dirty water back on the floor.

For dirtier floors, use a mild, nonabrasive floor cleaner. Sponge the cleaner onto the floor and let it sit for several minutes to loosen the dirt. Then mop it up, scrubbing especially dirty areas and rinsing your mop frequently in a separate bucket.

Rinse the floor well to make sure you remove all the detergent, especially from no-wax floors, or a dingy film can build up. To prevent this, add up to 1 cup vinegar per gallon of rinse water.

No-wax floors shouldn't need waxing (get it?), but many folks apply some kind of wax, polish, or finish anyway. After a while, this can become dingy, often because the old finish was not completely cleaned before a new finish was laid down on top of it. To strip wax and polish off floors, try our HomeMade Floor Wax Remover (at right).

For quick cleanup of everyday spills, spray the spill with our HomeMade General-Purpose Cleaner (page 43) and let sit for a few minutes. (Be wary of stronger cleaning agents, which can remove wax from the floor or even damage the finish.) Then scrub with a

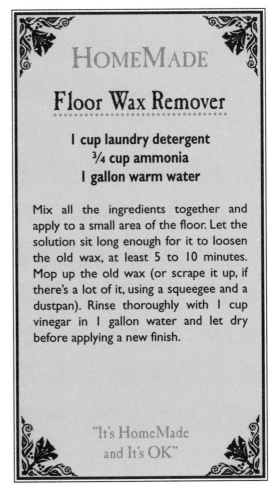

HomeMade

Floor Wax Remover

1 cup laundry detergent
¾ cup ammonia
1 gallon warm water

Mix all the ingredients together and apply to a small area of the floor. Let the solution sit long enough for it to loosen the old wax, at least 5 to 10 minutes. Mop up the old wax (or scrape it up, if there's a lot of it, using a squeegee and a dustpan). Rinse thoroughly with 1 cup vinegar in 1 gallon water and let dry before applying a new finish.

"It's HomeMade and It's OK"

sponge or, for heavier spills, use a plastic ice scraper, which won't mar vinyl floors.

Another old-fashioned trick is to slice an orange in half and use the two halves, one in each hand, to scrub the floor. The citric acid in the orange will cut through grease and dirt on the floor.

Candles   See Wax (page 93).

Crayon   Our HomeMade General-Purpose Cleaner (page 43) will often remove crayon marks from floors. To remove your child's more aggressive artistic creations, try an old toothbrush dipped in paste wax, silver polish, or even toothpaste (not the gel type). If you don't have an old toothbrush, a damp rag will do.

 Hot fat
When hot fat falls on the floor, pour cold water on it at once, and it will harden so that it can be easily removed with a knife. (1911)

Odors   To remove odors from floors, sprinkle the area with baking soda, let sit, then vacuum. The stronger the odor, the more soda you should use and the longer you should leave it on.

Pet accidents   To clean up your pet's accidents, see the tips for carpets (page 88). One trick to try on bare floors is to place a slice of onion on the spot after cleaning, which should give Fido or Fluffy the message that this isn't the potty.

Salt   To clean up rock salt tracked in on boots during the winter, mop with a mixture of equal parts vinegar and water.

Scuff marks   Black scuff marks from shoes and boots can often be removed from floors with our HomeMade General-Purpose Cleaner (page 43). Spray it on, let sit, and then scrub gently with a nylon-backed sponge.

For floors with heavier marks (or many of them), mix ¼ cup trisodium phosphate (available at hardware stores) and 2 gallons hot water and wash the floor with this. Trisodium phosphate is fairly strong stuff, so use it carefully. You may have to rewax afterward.

Other solvents such as alcohol can remove scuff marks but may remove wax as well, so test the solvent in a corner before going wild with it.

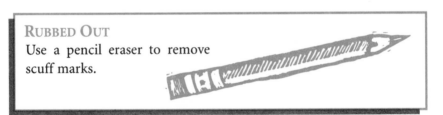

RUBBED OUT
Use a pencil eraser to remove scuff marks.

Tar   Soften tar on floors by working vegetable oil into it with your fingers, then cleaning it up with our HomeMade General-Purpose Cleaner (page 43).

A friend of ours found that she was able to remove tar from her freshly waxed floor by scrubbing it with scrunched-up wax paper.

Wax   Put some ice cubes in a plastic sandwich bag and place the bag on the wax for 10 to 15 minutes. Then chip or scrape away the frozen wax with a dull knife. Use our HomeMade General-Purpose Cleaner (page 43) to remove any remaining color, or try one of the tips under Crayon (page 92).

Chapter 6

Indoor Cleaning

I N 1876, *THE OLD FARMER'S ALMANAC* OPINED THAT "the simple want of order and neatness is enough of itself to make home repulsive, especially to children brought under the influence of it; and every parent ought to realize this fact."

It may be too much to expect our houses to be orderly — that's a subject for another book altogether — but most of us would like to have a neat house. There are several ways to achieve this:

■ Inviting friends over

■ Deciding never to have children

■ Moving to a brand-new house

If these and other tactics seem too drastic or don't have the desired effect, take solace in the adage "Cleanliness is next to impossible."

CLOSETS

Beyond the accumulation of junk, the major cleaning task for closets seems to be the three *m*s: moisture, mildew, and mustiness. Here are a few ways to deal with them.

- The most effective (and, unfortunately, most expensive) method is to run an air conditioner or dehumidifier, which will remove excess moisture from the air.

- For small closets and bathrooms, place a bag of silica or other absorbent material, available at most hardware stores, in the space.

- Make your own moisture absorber by placing charcoal briquettes in a coffee or powdered-drink can with a plastic top. Punch holes in the top to allow air to circulate around the briquettes. If that seems like too much work, just put the charcoal in a shallow pan on the floor.

- A light left on in a small closet or bathroom will sometimes give off just enough heat to keep the room dry.

- To freshen the air in a closet, place some cedar chips in a nylon stocking or mesh bag and hang it from the closet pole. The cedar also will discourage moths from moving in.

DUSTING & VACUUMING

For general-purpose dusting, old terry cloth hand towels are ideal. The irregular surface picks up dust better than smooth cloths, and they are sturdy enough to withstand abuse and washing. A bit of moisture from a spray mister will make dust cloths pick up dust better.

 Pour a little oil or water on one end of your cloth duster; roll it up and wring until the water or oil has spread over the whole. This will prevent the flying of the light dust over adjacent articles. (1912)

A windshield brush (the kind used to brush snow off your car in winter) also makes a good duster for those hard-to-reach places.

A good vacuum cleaner is worth its weight in gold. Here are some tips to get the most out of yours.

- Vacuum early and often. The more dust you remove from your house, the fewer dust particles (and allergens and pollen grains) will be recycled from room to room by traffic and air currents.

- Change the vacuum bag often to keep the vacuum working at its peak efficiency.

- Check the roller brush attachment each time you use it to remove hairs, strings, and elastic bands that can wrap around the bar. A small pair of scissors makes it easy to remove these.

- To freshen the air as you vacuum, sprinkle a few drops of lemon juice or some cinnamon into the bag. Or use our HomeMade Carpet Freshener (page 117).

Radiators   Place a damp cloth on the back side and blow through the radiator with a hair dryer set on high or your vacuum cleaner hose attached to the outlet vent.

Tight spots   To clean underneath or behind refrigerators, furniture, or other large objects, place an old sock or stocking over a yardstick and attach it with rubber bands. This also works for reaching cobwebs in corners.

Tiny spots   A clean one- or two-inch paintbrush is ideal for dusting small or uneven surfaces such as picture frames, lampshades, light fixtures, and between piano keys.

Beyond the Broom

You think your house is a mess? Consider this: The White House was built in the early 1800s, but the first commercial vacuum cleaner wasn't introduced until 1907. That means the First Rugs weren't vacuumed for 90 years.

Before the invention of mechanical cleaning devices, homemakers and harried servants carried rugs and carpets outside, hung them over lines, and attacked them with rug beaters that looked like paddles for some strange outdoor game — a process that was about as much fun as it sounds.

In between spring cleanings, housekeepers did the best they could with a round broom, a device that had been in existence since biblical times and hadn't changed much since then. The Shakers are credited with inventing the flat broom, stitching the bristles into a shape that sweeps a wider path and reaches into corners more easily. But it was a cylindrical broom, that led to the next great innovation in cleaning technology.

In 1699, a British inventor named Edmund Heming devised a contraption for cleaning London's streets. The device consisted of a large circular brush pulled by a horse-drawn cart, which, according to complaining Londoners, spewed more dust than it picked up.

Later inventors borrowed the revolving-brush concept, attempting to create a mechanical broom for indoor use. But early carpet sweepers were clunky, didn't work very well, and received a cool reception from the average homemaker.

Among the folks who weren't happy with the mechanical sweepers of the day were Melville and Anna Bissell, who sold crockery and glassware from a small shop in Grand Rapids, Michigan. The Bissells waged a never-ending battle against dust and debris from the straw in which their glassware was shipped.

In 1876, determined that he could create a better carpet sweeper, the mechanically inclined Melville created his own

➤➤

sweeper, with a handmade walnut case, hog-bristle brushes, and "certain new and useful improvements" for cleaning uneven surfaces better than earlier models.

The Bissells' new carpet sweeper sounded like a threshing machine, but it worked like a charm. Customers asked about it, and soon the Bissells were selling more sweepers than saucers. They gave up glassware to form the Bissell Carpet Sweeper Company, and within a few years the name Bissell had become synonymous with the carpet sweeper. A common expression of the time even referred to carpet sweeping as "Bisselling the carpet."

The problem with a carpet sweeper is that it works only on dirt big enough for its brushes to pick up. In the search for a device that would pick up smaller particles, inventors came up with hundreds of odd devices. Some, designed to blow dirt off rugs and into a collection container, simply redistributed the dust around the room. Other devices used suction to pick up dirt. These included bellows-shaped devices that drew in air rather than blowing it out and gadgets that looked like a bug sprayer or bicycle pump and were pumped along a shaft to create a

vacuum. Many were hand-held devices, but there were larger floor models that required two people to operate them: one to pump and the other to direct the cleaning nozzle.

When the dust settled, the patent for the first successful mechanical vacuum cleaner went to a Chicago inventor named Ives W. McGaffey. McGaffey patented his hand-powered "suction sweeper" in 1869 and sold it under the trade name Whirlwind. The Whirlwind's career was short-lived, however, as most of McGaffey's inventory was destroyed in the Chicago Fire of 1871. Today only a few of his cleaners remain in existence.

By the close of the 19th century, electric gadgets for the home began springing up. The electric fan, oven, sewing machine, and iron were all created within a ten-year span. It was only a matter of time before inventors began attaching motors to vacuum cleaners. The first efforts were less than electrifying.

In England, an engineer named Hubert C. Booth witnessed a demonstration of a carpet cleaner that used compressed air to blow dust into a container. Unimpressed, Booth was convinced that suction was a better method for cleaning. But how to keep dirt and dust from clogging the motor? Using his mouth to provide suction (and nearly choking to death in the process), Booth began experimenting with filters to trap dirt and dust while allowing air to pass through. The result was the first vacuum cleaner bag, with a motor that drew air through it into a collection container.

Booth's electric vacuum cleaner, patented in 1901, worked magnificently. The problem was its size: the cleaner was as large as a refrigerator, requiring a horse-drawn dolly to transport it and two people to operate it. Few people could afford to own one, so Booth started a cleaning service that went from house to house and business to business sucking up centuries of dirt. Among his early clients was Westminster Abbey, where Booth cleaned the rugs prior to the coronation of Edward VII — the first time they'd been vacuumed in the church's 900-year history!

Among average people, however, Booth's electric vacuum was no more popular than Heming's mechanical sweeper had been 200 years earlier. Aside from its cost was the noise of the motor, which was reportedly so loud it caused horses to bolt in the street. The general public would not embrace the electric vacuum cleaner until an American, an aging janitor with sinus problems, came up with a smaller, portable device.

James Murray Spangler was a custodian in Canton, Ohio. He was afflicted with a severe allergy to dust, a condition that was only worsened by the carpet sweeper he used on the job. Anxious to save his sinuses and his job, Spangler rigged up a motor from an electric fan, a soapbox, a broomstick, and a pillowcase to create the first portable electric vacuum cleaner. The device worked so well that Spangler patented it in 1907 and began selling it as the Electric Suction Sweeper.

Spangler's fortune was made when he sold a cleaner to a woman whose husband manufactured harnesses and leather goods. The manufacturer recognized a good thing when he saw it and purchased the rights to sell the new machine. He named it after himself, and the cleaner sold like hotcakes, making the manufacturer's name — Hoover — a household word.

ELECTRONIC EQUIPMENT

All the electronic devices in your home are magnets for fingerprints and dust. In some cases, the dirt can do them harm, but cleaning needs to be undertaken with caution as well. Add these items to your occasional cleaning list and follow the tips below.

Camera   If you're a photographer and you have a camera that's expensive enough to worry about, you probably already know this: clean your camera's lens by blowing dust off with compressed air (available at camera and audio stores) or using lens cleaner and cleaning paper. Never touch the surface of the lens, and never use any other cleaning solution.

Compact discs & CD player   Have you ever had a compact disc start skipping? We have, and nine times out of ten, if you turn the disc over to look at the shiny side, where the music is recorded, you'll see a speck of dirt (or perhaps a big, disgusting fingerprint). Sometimes that's all it takes to make a CD misplay.

To clean a compact disc, use a clean, lint-free cloth. Moisten it with warm water and very, very gently rub the disk in a straight line from the center to the edge. (Note that this is exactly the opposite of the way you should clean records.) You can also purchase commercial cleaning kits for compact discs, but we've been able to rescue most discs just with warm water.

Clean the outside of your CD player with our HomeMade General-Purpose Cleaner (page 43) or our HomeMade Glass Cleaner (page 113). To clean the laser that plays the disc, you'll need to buy a cleaning CD, which is essentially a tiny brush mounted to a disc. Use this occasionally to clear airborne dust from the player's lens. (This is the equivalent of cleaning your record player's stylus.)

Computer   Clean the outside of your computer with our HomeMade General-Purpose Cleaner (page 43) or our HomeMade Glass Cleaner (page 113). Always spray the cleaner on the cleaning cloth, not on the unit itself.

The nature of computer screens makes them dust magnets. You can clean them with ordinary cleaners, but an antistatic cleaner (available at audio or computer stores) will keep dust away longer. Again, spray the cleaner on the cloth, not directly on the screen.

Those of us who open up our computers occasionally are often dismayed at the amount of dust that finds its way inside. A hand-held mini vacuum cleaner is ideal for cleaning inside the computer, but they're expensive. We made our own using an old vacuum attachment and duct-taping a piece of flexible plastic tubing (available at most hardware stores) to it in an airtight fashion. This provides plenty of suction power and lets you reach around inside where the dust may be lurking. Make sure the computer is off, and avoid touching the components as you're vacuuming, to prevent any electricity from zapping your system.

Clean around the computer keys with a clean cotton swab or toothbrush. To remove built-up grunge, dip the swab or brush in rubbing alcohol and scrub gently. If your keyboard is extremely dirty, you can actually wash it. We discovered this after spilling a cup of coffee on a keyboard. This isn't something you want to do every day, but in case of emergencies, it can be a lifesaver.

■ Turn off the computer and unplug the keyboard before the spill has time to dry.

■ Turn the keyboard over and remove the screws that hold the cover on. Carefully disconnect the keyboard cord and remove the inside of the keyboard.

■ Put just enough warm water in your sink to cover the inside of the keyboard. Soak the keyboard for 15 to 30 minutes. If the keyboard is extremely grungy, leave it in longer.

■ Remove the keyboard from the sink and shake it gently to get rid of as much water as possible.

■ Rinse gently under cool, running water, then air-dry completely before reassembling.

Photocopier   Clean the glass plate of the office photocopier with a paper coffee filter. In contrast to paper towels, coffee filters are lint free.

Records   Remember records? If you still have them (or collect them), the tool described below, or an expensive audio store version of the same thing, is still the best way to clean them. Be sure to clean *with* the grooves.

 To dust records of a talking machine, fasten a piece of velvet over a block of wood and brush the record with a rotary movement. (1922)

Occasionally, old records can actually become mildewed from being stored in a damp place. To remove mildew, hold the record by the edges and dampen it with cold water (try to avoid the label as much as possible). Squirt a bit of mild dishwashing liquid on your fingers and rub along the record, working with the grooves, not across them. Once both sides are thoroughly cleaned, rinse again under cold water. Dry with a clean chamois or record cloth (available at audio stores).

Commercial record-cleaning kits also are available. We've even cleaned old records by using rubbing alcohol on a soft cloth, with no ill effects.

To clean your record player itself, dust with a soft, clean cloth and our HomeMade Glass Cleaner (page 113) if necessary. Avoid using oily cleaners on plastic surfaces. Clean the record stylus with a soft brush, brushing from front to back (not side to side) so as not to bend it.

BRUSH UP YOUR STEREO

If you're looking for a tiny brush to clean electronic parts such as a record stylus, try an old mascara brush. Before using, soak it in a mixture of 1 cup warm water and 1 tablespoon ammonia to remove the mascara completely, then dry.

Tape recorder & player

Tape recorders build up dirt and magnetism that need to be removed occasionally. Commercial demagnetizers and cleaning tapes are available, or you can clean your   recorder's heads and the transport mechanism using a cotton swab dipped in denatured alcohol. Allow to dry completely before using the recorder again.

Telephone A cotton swab dipped in alcohol works well to clean around the buttons on a telephone (or under the dial plate if you still have a rotary phone). During cold and flu season, it's also a good idea to clean the whole phone with a cloth dampened with alcohol. Pay special attention to the area around the mouthpiece, as this is a likely place for germs to be transmitted from one family member to another.

VCR Use our HomeMade General-Purpose Cleaner (page 43) or our HomeMade Glass Cleaner (page 113) on the outside of your video player. As with a CD player, you'll need to purchase a cleaning tape to clean the inside of the system. One of the best ways to keep the heads clean is to use only high-quality recording tapes. Cheap tapes can shed tiny bits of metal that will eventually collect on the recording head.

ELECTRONIC COVER-UP

If dust is a problem in your home (and where isn't it?), protect electronic devices by covering them with a plastic cover when not in use. The little bit of time it takes to remove the cover will be worth it in terms of longer equipment life.

Dust to Dust

Dust is everywhere, and any attempt to rid your life of it is as futile as running away from yourself.

Ever wonder what's in that dust gathering around your knickknacks, layering Aunt Edna's Louis XIV dining table, and collecting on your dust rag and in your vacuum cleaner? If you must know, it's *you.* Household dirt and dust are made up mostly of human skin cells, flaked off by the millions. Each human produces about a pound of this stuff per year! And if that's not disgusting enough, the remaining dust is made up of hair, animal dander, pollen, cosmic dust, salt from the ocean, carbon from smoke, volcanic ash, cigarette smoke, cooking residue, bacteria, viruses, mold spores, insect debris (bodies, eggs, and droppings), and last, but certainly not least, dust mites and their fecal matter.

There are plenty of reasons to hate dust, but mostly we do because it makes us look like bad housekeepers, even when we're reasonably clean folks. Dust likes to huddle together in the quiet places of your home —

under your furniture and behind objects, where little dust bunnies hold conventions and secret meetings. Dust especially likes the things in your home that are good at blowing it around, such as radiators, heat registers, and wood-burning stoves. Think of these places as "park and ride" lots for dust. Vacuuming them diligently will help control the dust population in your home.

Once dust has hitched a ride, it likes to hang out in carpeting, bedding, upholstered furniture, and dust-catching decorations, so another way to control dust in your home is to cover or eliminate those areas as much as possible. Encase your mattresses in plastic and have as few overstuffed chairs, heavy draperies, and deep carpets as possible. Go with hardwood floors, and clean them religiously.

Another reason to hate dust is that many of us are allergic to it (which, given its omnipresence, is a little like saying we are allergic to air). We sneeze, wheeze, and get itchy eyes or congested sinuses. Dust is everywhere, nearly impossible to avoid entirely unless you live in a bubble or take up residence in Antarctica, where you'd probably still be producing your share of flaking skin but nobody would come to visit, so you wouldn't have to care about dusting.

People with allergies to dust are actually allergic to the fecal matter produced by the dust mites that love to nibble on dust. There can be as many as 2,000 dust mites in an ounce of dust, so it's not like you can politely ask them to leave your home. The standard medical treatment for a dust allergy is a series of inoculations, a process that can be lengthy and expensive and that may not yield lifelong results. Most folks make do with over-the-counter antihistamines and decongestants.

FLOOR TOOL TIPS

To keep your dust mop cleaning efficiently, vacuum it thoroughly after each use. (Store the vacuum near the mop to encourage yourself to do this.)

If you'd rather shake the dust out of your mop but don't want the dust flying back at you, place the mop head in a large plastic bag and fasten the bag to the handle with a rubber band. Shake well and then discard the bag.

Wash the mop head occasionally by tossing it in a plastic mesh bag (the kind onions come in), tying it up, and throwing it in the washing machine.

When changing the bag in your vacuum cleaner, do it over a newspaper that you've sprinkled lightly with water. The dampness will help keep the dust from flying around, and you can roll the whole mess up and throw it away afterward.

Sprinkling a bit of water on your carpet sweeper brush will make it a better dust collector. A spray bottle that makes a fine mist is great for this.

FURNITURE

Glass tabletops   Clean glass tabletops with our HomeMade Glass Cleaner (page 113). Use a terry cloth towel to buff dry.

Small scratches on a glass tabletop can sometimes be removed by buffing with toothpaste (not the gel type).

Leather   Leather upholstery and desktops should be cleaned with a damp cloth and saddle soap (or some other fine soap, such as castile soap). Use as little water as possible and dry well, since water can make leather dry and brittle.

If wax builds up on leather desktops from too much polishing, use 1 tablespoon vinegar in 1 cup warm water to remove it. Buff dry, and thereafter use lemon oil to condition the leather.

White rings and spots left on leather by water spills can sometimes be removed with petroleum jelly. Cover the spot with jelly and let sit for 1 to 2 days. Remove the jelly with a soft, clean cloth and buff.

To kill mildew on leather, wipe it down with a mixture of equal parts alcohol and water.

Metal   Before painting metal furniture (such as an old iron bed), clean it by washing it down with vinegar. The vinegar will evaporate, so you don't need to rinse it off.

To remove iron rust, mix fine salt and cream of tartar, moisten with water, and lay on the stain. Expose to the sun, and repeat the application if necessary. (1874)

You can also remove rust from metal furniture with turpentine or a commercial rust remover containing oxalic acid (available at hardware stores).

Upholstery   Upholstered furniture should be vacuumed regularly to remove the dust and dirt that can settle into the fabric.

For quick cleanup of stains on upholstery, try shaving cream (which sticks to horizontal surfaces such as chair legs and backs). Spray a small amount on the stain and gently work it in with your fingers or a soft brush. Sponge away with a clean, damp cloth, blotting to dry. Repeat if necessary until the stain is gone.

For advice on removing specific stains from upholstery, see the sections on stain removal for laundry (page 70) and carpeting (page 83).

A bit of moisture on a cleaning rag or chamois will help pick up pet hairs on sofas and chairs. Spray the cloth lightly with a mister and pass it quickly over the fabric.

Vinyl & plastic   Clean vinyl furniture with warm water and a mild dishwashing liquid, or try our HomeMade General-Purpose Cleaner (page 43).

To remove spots from vinyl furniture, put a little baking soda or toothpaste (not the gel type) on a damp cloth and scrub.

You can also use vinegar to remove spots from vinyl.

To put a quick polish on vinyl or plastic furniture, use automotive paste wax. Apply it sparingly and buff to a shine.

Wicker   To keep wicker furniture from drying out, clean it occasionally with a little furniture polish or vegetable oil sprinkled on a soft brush.

Outdoor wicker furniture can become mildewed if put away while wet or stored in a damp place. To remove mildew from wicker, wash it with a mixture of vinegar and water (up to straight vinegar for bad cases of mildew). Use a brush to remove mildew from all the crevices. Dry well before storing.

Another mildew remover is warm salt water. Wash the wicker, rinse, and dry well.

Wood   For general cleaning and polishing, use our HomeMade Furniture Polish (below).

Another classic cleaning method for varnished furniture is to use leftover tea (or brew a strong solution and let it cool). Soak a clean cloth in it and use this to wipe down the finish.

Paper & decals   Tape, decals, and other paper that's stuck on wooden furniture (or other wooden items such as picture frames) will come off if you cover the paper with vegetable oil. Let the oil sit for a few minutes, then peel off the paper and remove any remaining residue with vinegar and water or our HomeMade Furniture Polish (this page).

You can also use vinegar to remove decals and labels. Dampen the paper with vinegar and let it sit for a couple of minutes, then peel or gently scrape off. Vinegar also works to remove glue spilled on furniture.

Rings & spots   Methods for removing rings left on wood by damp glasses are plentiful. Try these until you find one that works for you.

Cover the ring with petroleum jelly and leave it on for 24 hours, then wipe it off.

Make a paste of salad oil and salt and apply this to the ring. Let sit for 1 to 2 hours before wiping off.

Apply toothpaste (not the gel type) or baking soda to a damp cloth and rub the ring until it's gone. Remove the paste with a clean cloth.

HomeMade

Furniture Polish

1 tablespoon vinegar or lemon juice
1 tablespoon boiled linseed oil
1 tablespoon turpentine

Combine the ingredients in a glass jar with a tight-fitting lid and shake until blended. Dampen a cloth with cold water and wring it out until it's as dry as you can get it. Saturate the cloth with the mixture and apply sparingly to a small area at a time. Let dry for about 30 minutes, then polish with a soft cloth. Note that this mixture gets gummy as it sits, so make just enough for one day's work.

"It's HomeMade
and It's OK"

White spots may be removed from furniture by placing over them a cloth dipped in almost boiling water and then rubbing them with a dry soft cloth, repeating the operation if necessary. (1904)

Scuff marks   Scuff marks can accumulate on the legs of tables, chairs, and other furniture pieces where they bump up against each other. To remove them, dip a piece of the finest-grade (0000) steel wool in vegetable oil. Rub the scuff marks gently until they disappear. Be careful not to mar the finish.

Stains   To remove stains from bare wood, paint them with a mixture of equal parts bleach and water. If the stains are severe, you can use straight bleach.

A rust remover containing oxalic acid (available at hardware stores) also can be used to remove some stains from wood.

Wax   To remove built-up wax from wooden furniture, rub the surface with a mixture of equal parts vinegar and water on a clean cloth. Dry immediately with another cloth.

For really heavy wax buildup, use paint thinner, but apply only as much as you need and wipe it off quickly so that you don't damage the finish.

You can also remove old wax by warming it with a hair dryer and rubbing it down with paper towels or a clean cloth.

POLISHING CLOTHS

You can make your own polish-impregnated cloths to dust furniture. Pour some furniture polish into a large glass jar and shake it until the sides are coated. Pour the remainder of the polish back into the polish container. Place terry or other absorbent cloths in the jar and cover tightly. Leave overnight or until the cloths have absorbed all the polish. Store the cloths in the jar.

Here's another method for making polishing cloths. Add ¼ cup polish (such as lemon oil) to 2 cups hot water. Mix well. Soak dust cloths in the mixture, then let them dry before using. Save the mixture in a glass jar. When the cloths become soiled, wash them, re-treat them, and use again.

WALLS

Paint   For general-purpose cleaning of painted walls, mopboards, and other painted surfaces, combine ½ to 1 cup ammonia; ¼ cup baking soda, washing soda (available in the laundry section of supermarkets), or borax; and 1 gallon warm water. Mix thoroughly to dissolve the powder. Use the mixture to sponge down the walls, scrubbing marks gently. Since there's no soap or detergent in this mixture, you shouldn't have to rinse after washing (unless the ammonia smell is too strong for you).

Crayon   To remove crayon marks from painted walls, put a little baking soda on a damp cloth or sponge and scrub gently.

If this doesn't work, you may need to use a solvent such as lighter fluid or mineral spirits. Test in an inconspicuous spot to make sure the solvent won't remove the paint.

Marks   For marks that won't come off with the solution recommended for general cleaning of painted walls (above), many hardware stores sell something called a dry sponge, which you can rub over spots to remove them.

An art gum eraser will remove some marks on paint.

Wallpaper   If you have a good washable wallpaper, you can simply wash it with a mild dishwashing liquid in warm water. For cleaning large areas, use a sponge mop with a new head on it.

Following are some suggestions for removing marks and stains from wallpapered walls.

Grease   More than a hundred years ago, *The Old Farmer's Almanac* offered the following trick. It still works and is even easier thanks to electric irons with constant heat.

To remove grease from wallpaper, lay several folds of blotting paper on the spot and hold a hot iron near it until the grease is absorbed. (1888)

Another way to remove grease spots from wallpaper is to dust them with talcum powder, let sit for a couple of hours, and brush off. Cornstarch or borax also can be used for this.

Marks Marks on wallpaper that can't be washed away will often come off with a gum eraser (available at most art supply stores). Gum erasers crumble as you use them and are less likely to smear a mark than regular pencil erasers.

If you don't have a gum eraser handy, try rubbing marks and grease stains with a piece of stale bread. (Why stale? Because if it isn't stale, you should eat it.) The bread acts as a gentle abrasive, although it's crumbly, so keep your dustpan or mini vacuum cleaner handy.

Stains Remove stains from wallpaper with a mild solvent (such as dry-cleaning fluid or rubbing alcohol). Test in an inconspicuous spot to be sure the solvent doesn't damage the wallpaper.

Tape Remove tape and other adhesives from wallpaper by passing a warm iron over them to melt the glue, then gently peel off. Use a mild dishwashing liquid in warm water to remove any glue that remains on the wall.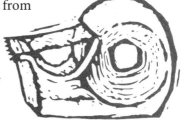

WINDOWS

Over the years, *The Old Farmer's Almanac* has offered many solutions for cleaning windows. The 1904 edition suggested, "If the water used in cleaning windows is blued, they will retain their brightness longer and polish more easily." The next year, the Almanac noted, "Mortar and paint may be removed from window glass with hot, sharp vinegar."

 Windows can be cleaned in winter and the frost entirely removed by using a gill [½ cup] of alcohol to a pint of hot water. (1912)

This recipe is essentially the same as automotive windshield washer, which you can also use to wash windows in cold weather (and which, in an example of "everything that's old is new again," is usually blue). Even in warm weather, the alcohol-water solution can be handy for removing grease or a smoky film from windows resulting from smoking or cooking.

For everyday window washing, try our HomeMade Glass Cleaner (page 113). Here are some general tips for washing windows.

■ Don't wash windows on sunny days. The sun will dry the window before you can adequately wipe or rinse the dirty solution off.

■ Wipe up and down on one side and side to side on the other. That way, if there are streaks, you'll be able to tell which side they're on.

■ Use soft, lint-free towels. Old terry cloth hand towels are perfect.

ALL THE NEWS THAT'S FIT FOR WASHING

If you've heard this suggestion once, you've heard it a thousand times (at least *we* have): use newspaper to clean your windows. Call us heretics, but we don't like the idea. First, newspaper isn't really all that absorbent, and it leaves your hands — and possibly the windowsills — with black smudges.

The obvious alternative, paper towels, can leave too much lint behind. Old terry cloth hand towels are perfect for washing windows, and they're reusable — just toss them in the washing machine occasionally to freshen them up. Leave the newspaper for starting fires or lining Polly's birdcage.

Tape residue   To remove tape residue from windows, use nail polish remover or another solvent. The solvent will evaporate, so you need not rinse. If you don't have a solvent handy, use vegetable oil to loosen the glue. You'll have to wash the oil and glue off afterward.

Venetian blinds   To wash venetian blinds without removing them, put on a pair of soft cotton work gloves. Dip your hands in a bucket of warm, soapy water and use your fingers to clean the slats of the blind. Then dip your hands in a bucket of clean water. Repeat until the entire blind is clean.

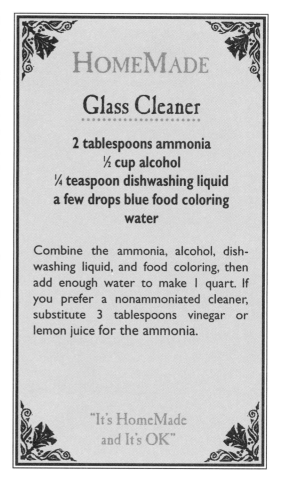

HomeMade

Glass Cleaner

**2 tablespoons ammonia
½ cup alcohol
¼ teaspoon dishwashing liquid
a few drops blue food coloring
water**

Combine the ammonia, alcohol, dishwashing liquid, and food coloring, then add enough water to make I quart. If you prefer a nonammoniated cleaner, substitute 3 tablespoons vinegar or lemon juice for the ammonia.

"It's HomeMade
and It's OK"

You can also hang venetian blinds from your clothesline and use the sprayer attachment on your garden hose to wash them. Scrub any spots with a soapy sponge, then rinse with the hose.

If your shower has a detachable head, hang the blinds in the shower and spray them. (This is easier to do if you're showering yourself at the time!)

If you don't have a clothesline or shower, fill your child's wading pool with warm water and a mild dishwashing liquid. Soak the blinds for a few minutes, empty the pool, refill with clean warm water, and rinse. Hang the blinds to dry. Be sure to rinse the pool thoroughly. (You can also do this in your bathtub, but be careful not to scratch the tub's surface.)

The House of the Future

We have automatic clothes washers, dishwashers, and carpet cleaners (among other amenities). Does it get any better than that? How about a house that is entirely self-cleaning?

The self-cleaning house is the brainchild and working laboratory of Frances Gabe, now an octogenarian inventor. Every room in the house is rigged with an overhead system that hoses down and then blow-dries everything in it. Sound about as cozy as living in a car wash? It *is* cozy, because Gabe has thought of everything. She has invented an upholstery fabric that repels water. Her books are equipped with a plastic cover that shuts automatically if the book is forgotten on the coffee table. Her collection of antique furniture, including a 200-year-old bed, is protected with eight coats of the highest-grade marine varnish.

The cleaning process is this: (1) push the button; (2) leave the room while the detergent and water mixture is spraying; (3) come back in about 45 minutes, when all has been blow-dried. The only thing Gabe has to do is shut the cupboards and cover her bedding with a sort of umbrella she's invented that pulls over it like a sheet. A drainage system channels the water and detergent from throughout the house to her living room, where it runs out through her fireplace (thereby cleaning it as well).

As if that's not wonderful enough, Gabe has figured out how to clean clothes while they hang in the closet and dishes while they sit in the cupboards. Her toilet is self-cleaning, too, by virtue of being a dry toilet — sort of an indoor outhouse without the smell.

Gabe has obtained 32 separate patents for the inventions that make her self-cleaning house possible, including the building blocks and joists that form the foundation. Although some of her ideas might seem a bit wacky, they have generated intense interest from the media and folks considering how people may live in the future. Someday the self-cleaning house may be as commonplace as the vacuum cleaner and the dishwasher!

Chapter 7
Air, Heat & Light

ACCORDING TO THE 1886 EDITION OF *THE OLD FARMER'S Almanac*, "In eight hours' breathing a full-grown man spoils as much fresh air as seventeen three-bushel sacks could hold. If you were shut up in a room seven feet broad, seven feet long, and seven feet high, the door and windows fitting so tightly that no air could pass through, you would die, poisoned by your own breath, in a very brief time."

As unlikely as that might seem, modern houses with airtight construction, heating systems, and electric lighting systems are actually more prone to such a scenario. The following sections address cleaning concerns related to the major systems in your home.

AIR

Sprinkle a few drops of vanilla extract on a cotton ball and place it wherever odors might be a problem: in the kitchen, bathroom, or wastebaskets. Other fragrant oils, available at craft and health food stores, also can be used.

Place a dab of fragrant oil on a cool light bulb. When the bulb is turned on, its heat will release the scent into the room.

Sprinkle a few spices (cinnamon, nutmeg, and cloves) into a small pan of water and simmer on your kitchen stove or wood stove.

Place potpourri pots around your home. Revive them occasionally by sprinkling with apple, rose, or other scented oils.

Air conditioners, humidifiers & dehumidifiers   The machines we use to keep the air in our homes comfortable need cleaning, too. To prevent fungus from growing in one of these units, clean the

pans, drains, and filters occasionally with a mixture of ½ cup bleach and 1 quart water. To remove mineral depositfrom the tank, scrub them with a mixture of equal parts vinegar and water. Rinse well before restarting the unit.

Carpets   Use our HomeMade Carpet Freshener (below) to freshen the air while you vacuum.

For very quick cleanups, simply sprinkle baking soda, salt, or cornstarch on your rug, let it sit for a while, and then vacuum. Baking soda is also good for removing odors from carpets, as it neutralizes many smells.

 As a carpet cleaner, bran slightly dampened, thrown on the carpet, and then thoroughly swept out is unexcelled. Removes all dust and, being damp, prevents dust from flying. (1915)

Cooking odors   To remove cooking odors from the kitchen, boil 1 tablespoon vinegar in 1 cup water.

Dust   To reduce dust in the air, you have to remove it from rugs, carpets, upholstery, and other places. Vacuum frequently, put plastic covers on mattresses and bedding, and dust, dust, dust. For more hints on dust removal, see Dusting & Vacuuming (page 95).

Paint odors   The smell of fresh paint can be removed by putting out a dish of ammonia, vinegar, or even sliced onion in water. All will absorb the paint smell overnight.

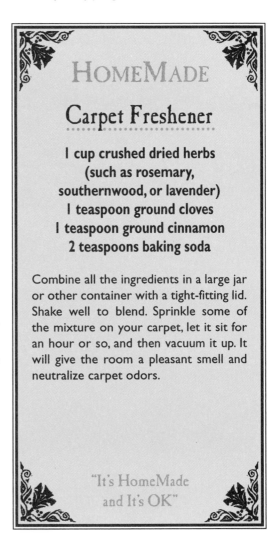

HOMEMADE

Carpet Freshener

**1 cup crushed dried herbs
(such as rosemary,
southernwood, or lavender)
1 teaspoon ground cloves
1 teaspoon ground cinnamon
2 teaspoons baking soda**

Combine all the ingredients in a large jar or other container with a tight-fitting lid. Shake well to blend. Sprinkle some of the mixture on your carpet, let it sit for an hour or so, and then vacuum it up. It will give the room a pleasant smell and neutralize carpet odors.

"It's HomeMade
and It's OK"

Smoke   If you have a smoke-free home but that lout
Uncle Harry lit up anyway, you can remove the smell
from the room by leaving a dish of ammonia out
overnight. If you allow smoking in your home
but want to contain it somehow, put bowls of
vinegar or charcoal briquettes where smokers
congregate to absorb the odor.

THE CASE FOR PLANTS

You may have heard that some houseplants — such as spider plant
and Chinese evergreen — can actually remove pollutants from the
air. In homes that are increasingly being made airtight to prevent
heat loss, fumes given off by cleaning agents, synthetic fibers, and
other sources are a real concern. Although some research
does indicate that plants can remove certain pollutants
from the air, the Environmental Protection Agency
points out that these tests were conducted under very
specific laboratory conditions. The only tests conducted in an actual building showed no benefit
from the use of plants. Nevertheless, we figure a few
plants can't hurt, and they may help. In the mean-
time, the best way to remove airborne pollutants
from your home is with good ventilation.

HEAT

Your heating system, whether electric, oil, or wood, contributes greatly to
the condition of your home. Here are some tips to keep the system and
your home cleaner and operating better.

Fireplaces & chimneys   It probably goes without saying that fireplace
chimneys need regular cleaning to avoid creosote buildup, which can
cause chimney fires. This cleaning isn't something most of us can do on
our own, and the "build a hot fire and burn it out" method is probably
responsible for a lot of new homes being built. Call a professional.

Ashes When cleaning the ashes out of your fireplace, first open the flue to encourage stray ashes to go up the chimney rather than into your living room. Use a kitty litter tray with a clean liner to collect the cold ashes. Remove the ashes by folding up the liner and discarding it.

 A good way to destroy the sooty smell sometimes found in a room when an open fireplace or grate has been closed for the summer is to make a fire of old newspapers and ground coffee. The coffee should be freely sprinkled among and over the newspapers before they are lighted. The heat extracts the aromatic qualities of the coffee, which purify the room, while the warmth engendered is fleeting. (1914)

Smudges   Soot and smoke smudges around your fireplace can be cleaned in a variety of ways. You should probably wear rubber gloves when using any of these cleaning methods. Also, avoid spilling the cleaning solutions on floors or rugs, and make sure the room is well ventilated.

Try an art gum eraser. Many stains can be removed with that.

You can also apply a paste of cream of tartar and water to the bricks. Rub it in, let it dry, and then scrub it off.

Here's another recipe for a solution that will take soot stains off most bricks. Dissolve ½ cup naphtha soap (available at hardware stores) in 1 quart hot water. Let cool, then stir in ½ cup ammonia and ½ pound powdered pumice. Apply to the bricks with a paintbrush. Let it soak in, scrub, and rinse with warm water.

Or you can combine ½ cup trisodium phosphate and 1 gallon water and scrub the bricks with it. (*Note:* Trisodium phosphate, available at hardware stores, is a strong substance, so use it carefully and wear rubber gloves while scrubbing.)

To clean white bricks, mix a solution of equal parts bleach and water in a spray bottle. Spray the bricks and scrub with a soft brush, then rinse with plain water.

Fireplace tiles with soot smudges can be cleaned with vinegar or washing soda (available in the laundry section of supermarkets).

Forced-hot-air furnace   Check your furnace filter at least once a month to see if it needs cleaning or changing. If dust accumulates near your furnace, clean it up to keep it out of circulation. An unsealed concrete floor in the furnace room can contribute to dust distribution throughout the house, so paint or seal the floor if possible.

Forced-hot-water radiators   Dust can accumulate inside baseboard hot-water heating systems. The copper tubing inside has "fins" that can get clogged, so vacuum these occasionally, using the upholstery brush attachment to keep from bending the fins.

To clean old-fashioned upright radiators, see the tip on page 96.

Wood stoves   A kitty litter tray with a clean liner works well to remove cold ashes from a wood stove, as described on page 119.

Dust the exterior of your wood stove with a cloth dampened with a bit of paint thinner. Avoid water on the dust rag, as you don't want the stove to rust. If your wood stove does rust, clean it with fine-grade (000 or 0000) steel wool and apply stove black or a fresh coat of stove paint.

LIGHT

Chandeliers   Use one part denatured alcohol mixed with three parts water to clean your chandelier. Put newspaper under the chandelier and dip each crystal into the solution. Or put the mixture in a spray bottle and spray the crystals, allowing them to drip onto the newspaper to dry.

Fluorescent lights   Small fluorescent light covers can be washed in the sink. To clean larger ones — such as those on shop lights — stand the covers in the bathtub, wash with our HomeMade General-Purpose Cleaner (page 43) and water, and let air-dry.

Lampshades   Lampshades are dust magnets. To blow away a light coating of dust, use a hair dryer set on low. You might want to do this outdoors to reduce the dust in your home.

A soft brush, such as an old shaving brush or a watercolor paintbrush, works well to clean pleated fabric shades.

If the dust is really bad, you might try giving your shade a shower, depending on the fabric. Blow-dry on low afterward.

Chapter 8
People & Pets

I N 1849, *THE OLD FARMER'S ALMANAC* NOTED, "A DIS-
tinguished writer upon health and longevity says, 'Extend the
same favor, daily, to your whole person, that you do to your
face and hands. All you require is two to five quarts of cold
water (and as much more as you please), and one or two
towels; the whole operation need not occupy five minutes. When you can
faithfully and fearlessly wash yourselves all over with cold water daily, you
will have taken a vast step in the commencement of uninterrupted health.'
The religion of some whom we call heathens enjoins this upon them,
while we, with all the lights of Christianity and civilization, are too apt to
neglect it."

Providing instructions and encouragement regarding bathing seems to us a bit like telling someone how to breathe, and yet bathing wasn't a regular occurrence in even our most recent past. Colonial Americans thought bathing to be injurious to one's health, as it removed precious oils that could stop the invasion of pestilence into the body. Most Americans these days bathe regularly, however, and our life expectancy seems not to have suffered for it.

Cleaning one's personal body parts is surely a personal matter, but media hype and advertising have influenced our perceptions of it. We seem to be too inclined to believe that what our forebears used couldn't possibly work on our modern, sensitive, and enlightened skins. In some cases, this is true. In others, we find that the return to "natural" and environmentally friendly personal care products is a return to our roots — in more ways than one.

Although some of us may gravitate toward high-priced personal care products — whether they be loofa sponges or brightly packaged mud packs from the rain forest — in the end the differences in most of these products are minuscule, and our choices come down to a matter of personal preference rather than conclusive scientific evidence that one product cleans better than another. Certainly, we want to avoid products that make us itchy or have a smell we don't care for, and some may in fact be too harsh for aging or sensitive skin. Deodorant soaps are, when you think about it, rather redundant and probably unnecessary except for people with the most excessive perspiration problems — whom we hope are showering frequently anyway.

In this chapter, we'll take a quick look at the "Big Four" of personal hygiene — face, hair, hands, and teeth — and then move on to some suggestions for minimizing the trauma associated with getting children and pets clean.

FACE

For women, the permutations in soaps, toners, clarifiers, emollients, exfoliants, and lotions to care for our skin are endless. Worse, just when you have a "routine" figured out, your skin changes and those products don't meet your needs anymore. (Men, on the other hand, just get to complain about shaving.) Following are some tips for treating your face gently.

Acne   Here's a home remedy for acne. Clean the face thoroughly, then pour a little apple cider vinegar into a basin of warm water. Splash your face thoroughly and let it air-dry. You can also spritz your face with vinegar, using a spray bottle.

If you have just one blemish sprouting on your otherwise perfect face, you can dry it up in a hurry by dabbing it with a bit of lemon juice a few times a day.

Dry skin   If you're plagued by very dry skin on your face (or dead skin on your feet, elbows, or knees), dip into the refrigerator and take out your bottle of Miracle Whip. (No, mayonnaise won't do, although it will work as a hair conditioner; see page 126.) Rub in a small amount, let it dry a bit, and then massage.

Facial mask   A wonderful, inexpensive facial mask is dry oatmeal — the kind that sticks to your ribs on a cold winter morning. Just take whole oats and grind them into a fine powder using your food processor or an electric coffee grinder. Make sure the oats are very finely ground, or this process will be messy. Keep the powder in a sealed container. When you're ready to use it, put 1 tablespoon of the powder in a small bowl and add enough water to make a slightly runny paste. Spread it in a thin film over your face, even down your neck if you like, avoiding the delicate area around your eyes. Let the paste dry (it won't take long), then rinse with warm water. Splash afterward with cool water. This treatment, used about every three days, makes some of the roughest skin feel smooth.

Makeup remover   Remove waterproof makeup by applying a little mineral oil or petroleum jelly with a cotton ball or soft facial sponge. Don't use facial tissues, as they can be too rough on the skin. In a pinch, a little vegetable or olive oil will work well, too, if you keep it out of your eyes. Vegetable oil also softens and moisturizes the skin.

Three-Step Beauty Treatment

Beauty consultants these days love to talk about exfoliating your skin (which sounds like something you'd do to an enemy in war). If you'd rather not pay beauty spa prices ($50 and up on average), you can do your own deep-cleaning routine at home.

STEP 1: STEAM

Boil some water and pour it into a large mixing bowl. Add the juice of one-half lemon and a handful of any chopped fresh herb, such as rosemary, thyme, basil, or mint. Cover your hair, perhaps with a shower cap, hold your face about 12 inches from the water, and then cover your head and the bowl with a towel to trap the steam. Steam for 15 minutes. (This may have the added benefit of unclogging your sinuses!)

After steaming, rinse your face with very cold water to close the pores. You can also use your favorite toner at this point. Don't do the steaming more than once a week, as it will dry out your skin.

STEP 2: ASTRINGENT

For some skin types, it's best to follow a cleaning with an astringent. Astringents can be costly items when purchased over the counter or at a salon. Make your own astringent to tighten pores and remove excess oil using ½ lemon, thinly sliced; ½ orange, thinly sliced; and ¾ cup alcohol. Place the lemon and orange slices in a blender, add the alcohol, and blend until the fruits are pulverized, about 1 minute. Strain the astringent into a jar. It will keep for up to 6 months in the refrigerator.

STEP 3: MOISTURIZER

Most skin past the age of 25 needs to be moisturized after washing. One moisturizer that's overlooked these days is petroleum jelly. It may sound greasy, but it works. Mix the jelly with a little water, rub it in, and you will have smooth, soft skin and save bundles.

HAIR

Every shampoo claims to have a magic ingredient — something natural or exotic-sounding — but basically, they all do the same things. (Interestingly, those extra ingredients seem to magically and naturally raise the price of the product considerably.)

All shampoos have a detergent to remove oil and dirt. They also have additives such as conditioners to put back into your hair what the detergent took out. Shampoos for oily hair have more than the average amount of detergent, while those for dry hair have more than the average amount of conditioner.

Other additives to shampoos include preservatives and ingredients that improve the scent or help the foaming action (you don't need foam for clean hair, but apparently people have come to expect it). Some shampoos have additives that color hair slightly, such as highlighting blond strands. If a shampoo says it will make your hair "look fuller" or "be more manageable," it has an additive that will coat your hair and make it thicker. This is probably not a good thing for many hair types, as coated hair also attracts more dirt and oil and hence requires more shampooing. The only cure for split ends or damaged hair is to cut it off. Shampoos that appear to eliminate split ends contain some ingredient that merely sticks the two pieces of hair together. Similarly, dandruff shampoos may be a waste. Most dandruff problems can be handled by regular shampooing. In more severe cases, a dermatologist should be consulted, as it is not the hair, but the skin underneath, that's at fault.

The truth is most people can't tell one shampoo from another in a blind test, aside from smell. To prove this to yourself, try washing your hair with baby shampoo for a week and see if you or anybody else notices the difference. Or buy one of the dollar-a-gallon brands at the local discount store. If you're not ready to take such a drastic plunge, try diluting your expensive shampoo. It'll last longer and get your hair just as clean.

In the end, the best shampoo is the one you like, for whatever reason. Try our recipes for homemade shampoos. Maybe you'll stumble upon one that can replace that expensive salon brand.

Basic shampoo   Grate some castile soap, then mix it with water in a blender or food processor. Add ¼ cup olive, avocado, or almond oil and ½ cup distilled water. Blend well and use sparingly.

Conditioning treatment   To condition your hair naturally, apply ½ cup mayonnaise to dry, unwashed hair. Cover with a plastic bag and let sit for 15 minutes. Rinse a few times before shampooing thoroughly.

Dandruff treatment   Wet your hair, rub in a handful of baking soda, and rinse. This may make your hair feel drier than usual, but that will pass after a few weeks, when your normal oils adjust.

Dry shampoos   When regular shampooing is impossible, try this dry shampoo. Mix together 1 tablespoon salt and ½ cup cornmeal. Put it in a shaker bottle and sprinkle lightly onto your hair. Brush thoroughly to get rid of dirt and oil.

Baby powder and cornstarch can also be used as dry shampoos in the same way.

Rinses   A great cream rinse (conditioner) for your hair is a mixture of 1 teaspoon liquid fabric softener and 1 cup water. It will make hair soft and manageable.

HANDS

 After washing dishes, or any like work, wash the hands carefully and wipe dry. Then rinse thoroughly in [equal parts] vinegar and water. A bottle of the mixture should be kept handy. (1887)

Recent concern over outbreaks of communicable diseases caused by bacteria such as E. coli and salmonella have renewed public health interest in hand washing. Our mothers had the right idea when they told us to wash our hands before eating and after using the bathroom. That advice stands today without exception. Besides protecting against more exotic (and possibly fatal) diseases, hand washing is the best way to avoid colds and flu, because germs that cause those illnesses are passed from one person's hands to another's, then enter the body through the nose, mouth, or eyes.

Sometimes, however, our hands suffer from so much washing, as well as from the effects of cleaners, detergents, household tasks, and just being in hot water frequently. They are the workhorses of the body – constantly in use and constantly abused. Here are some tips for taking care of your hands.

Odors   Preparing fish can leave your hands smelly long after dinner is over. Fresh lemon juice will take the smell out of your hands. Bottled lemon juice will work pretty well, too. (But don't try either if you have any cuts on your hands.)

Another method of removing the smell of fish, onion, or garlic from your hands is to sprinkle baking soda on them, work in a little water, scrub, and rinse. If the odor persists, repeat this procedure until it is gone.

Rubbing your hands with salt water is also a good deodorizer.

Paint   Use vegetable, baby, or mineral oil to remove many types of paint from your hands easily and safely.

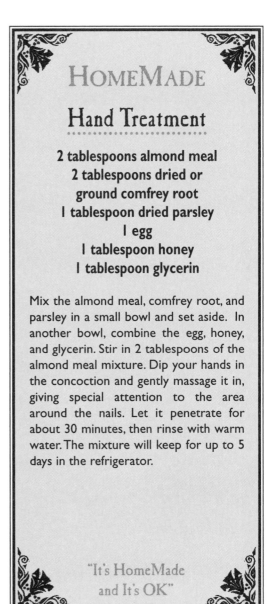

HomeMade

Hand Treatment

**2 tablespoons almond meal
2 tablespoons dried or
ground comfrey root
1 tablespoon dried parsley
1 egg
1 tablespoon honey
1 tablespoon glycerin**

Mix the almond meal, comfrey root, and parsley in a small bowl and set aside. In another bowl, combine the egg, honey, and glycerin. Stir in 2 tablespoons of the almond meal mixture. Dip your hands in the concoction and gently massage it in, giving special attention to the area around the nails. Let it penetrate for about 30 minutes, then rinse with warm water. The mixture will keep for up to 5 days in the refrigerator.

"It's HomeMade
and It's OK"

A HANDY ROAD TIP

If you're one of those people who always comes away from the self-serve gas pump smelling like a mechanic, you can keep the gas smell off your hands by donning a plastic sandwich bag before pumping. Keep a boxful in the glove compartment. If you're really serious about this, buy disposable latex gloves at your local pharmacy.

Stains

 It is an excellent thing to have a piece of fine pumice stone where it can be used readily, for it will remove ink and other stains from the fingers by merely wetting and rubbing over. Lemon juice is also useful for the same purpose, but should be carefully rinsed off, as the acid is drying to the skin. (1941)

Pumice is an amazing substance that has the same chemical composition as granite, yet with a density so low that it will float in water. Pumice is created when gas bubbles pass through molten lava, creating a foam that hardens. In solid form, pumice is useful for scrubbing mineral stains and calcification off hard, nonporous surfaces such as toilets and cast iron. Powdered pumice is used for polishing and as an abrasive in heavy-duty hand soaps.

Sticky stuff   A little vegetable oil will take sticky substances such as roofing tar or other petroleum-based products off your hands. Vegetable oil works better than paint thinner or mineral spirits and is nowhere near as harsh as those products on your skin.

Waterless cleaning   If you need to clean your hands but have no water (say, while camping), shaving cream is a good choice. It cleans and won't be sticky afterward.

TEETH

Perfect cleanliness will preserve the teeth to old age. How shall it be secured? Use a quill pick and rinse the mouth after eating. Brush [with] castile soap every morning, then brush with simple water on going to bed. Bestow this trifling care upon your precious teeth, and you will keep them and ruin the dentists. Neglect, and you will be sorry all your lives. (1873)

Methods for brushing your teeth seem to change right along with other trends. (That up-and-down motion you were taught in elementary school is no longer the preferred method, for example.) But here are some tips the professionals generally agree on — this week.

- Make sure you use a soft toothbrush.

- Brush gently, in small circular motions.

- Brush all the surfaces of your teeth and the gum line.

- Spend a full two minutes per brushing session.

- Change your toothbrush every three to four months.

- Adults should have a checkup and cleaning every six months, more if they are prone to plaque.

Denture cleaner   Make your own denture cleaner by combining 1 teaspoon water softener (available at drugstores), 1 teaspoon bleach, and

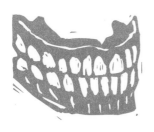

1 cup water. Soak your dentures in the solution for 10 to 15 minutes daily. Scrub with a denture brush and rinse well. Don't use this solution if you wear a partial denture that has any metal or wire on it.

CHILDREN

Any parent knows that the key to getting a young child clean without a lot of fuss and bother is to make it fun and, hopefully, instill the virtues of bathing at an early age so that he or she will *want* to bathe often. Bath time for very young children can be traumatic, and bathing mishaps are hard to forgive. ("You got soap in my eyes when I was three, and I'm never washing my hair again!") Here are some ways to reduce the stress.

Ear, ear!   For children who complain when you scrub the backs of their ears with a washcloth, use petroleum jelly instead. Rub some behind the ears, and they will be spotless the next day.

Gum be gone   To remove gum from your child's hair, place some ice cubes in a plastic sandwich bag, then freeze the gum by holding the bag to it. When the gum is frozen, break it up and chip it off.

Another gum-removal method is to work olive oil, peanut butter, or cold cream into the gum to loosen it, then (gently!) comb it out.

Mini shower   You can make rinsing off soap fun by keeping a watering can or pitcher in the bathroom. Use it to give your child a mini shower while he or she is sitting down.

Soapless eyes   To avoid the soap-in-the-eyes problem, have your child wear a tight-fitting underwater mask while you wash his or her hair. It's fun for the child and keeps the soap out of the eyes.

Another trick is to place petroleum jelly just over the child's eyebrows. This will keep soapy water from running into the eyes.

Soap sock   If you're using bar soap for your child's bath, put it inside a knotted-up sock. It'll be easier for the child to grab and use.

A TIP FOR NO TIPS

When kids are doing crafts with a bottle of paint or glue, cut a hole in a sponge and set the bottle in it. This keeps the bottle from tipping and soaks up any spills at the same time.

The Original All-Natural Cleaner

For many of us, the first cleaning solution we experienced was mother's spit. (Count yourself fortunate if you were one of the few kids whose mother did *not* spit on a hanky to clean your face just before you walked into church or grandma's house. A lot of us need a self-help group to get over this.)

Cleaner	pH
Oven cleaner	12–14
Ammonia (household)	11.9
Laundry detergent	8–12
Milk of magnesia	10.5
Baking soda solution	8.4
Saliva	7.4
Coffee	5.0
Vinegar	2.9
Cola	2.6
Lemon juice	2.3
Hydrochloric acid	0

It's not our mothers' fault, of course. It's genetic. Mothers have been cleaning their kids' faces with spit since ancient times. Traditionally, father's spit has not been used for cleaning, though no one seems to know why. Dad's spit seems to be reserved for tasks such as loosening a stubborn bolt or lubricating a fishing line.

Despite our initial traumatic exposure to it, mother's spit actually makes a fairly good cleaner. To begin with, saliva is mildly alkaline. Alkalinity and acidity are measured on a pH scale of 0 to 14. Anything below pH 7 is acidic, anything above is alkaline. Highly alkaline substances, such as oven cleaners and degreasers, are extremely caustic.

Mother's spit also contains enzymes, just like expensive detergents. The enzymes in saliva break down carbohydrates (making it perfect for removing dried jam from a child's face), as well as the cell walls of some bacteria (proof that mother's spit is actually antiseptic!).

Mother's spit is always handy, it's easily dispensed, and the price is right. So if you're an Adult Child of a Spit-Cleaning Mother, we have only one thing to say: get over it.

PETS

Pets are wonderful additions to any home — as long as they don't shed, have accidents, get sick, roll in anything foul, invite fleas home to dinner, or sleep on the beds. Since these are all included in the job descriptions of your average household pet, you and your furry friend may appreciate these tips.

We won't get into whether felines or canines make better pets or which are easier to live with. Suffice it to say that cats and dogs are certainly the most popular pets and present somewhat related cleaning challenges. Most of these tips work for either variety of household companion.

Burs   If Fido has been rolling in burs, use a pair of pliers to crunch them up, then rub in some vegetable, mineral, or baby oil to make them easier to remove.

Dog bath   If you bathe a dog in a bathtub, put a nylon hair net or stocking over the drain to catch the loose hairs.

A bit of baking soda in the rinse water will not only deodorize your pooch but also soften his fur. Vinegar or lemon juice will have the same effect, and it will ensure that all the soap is removed. Your own cream rinse (hair conditioner) may also benefit the dog's coat.

Fleas   If it's fleas you're after, you may be able to prevent future infestations by occasionally washing your dog or cat with salt water.

Feeding your pet a tablet of brewer's yeast and garlic may also keep fleas away.

Vacuum furniture and carpeting thoroughly during flea season, and use a flea comb on your cat or dog.

Another tactic is to clean your pet's favorite sleeping spots regularly and sprinkle them with fennel, rue, or rosemary to keep fleas at bay.

Hair   If you're just trying to live with the day-to-day hassles of pet ownership, hair can be a burden. Brush your pet often to remove loose hair. If your pet doesn't mind, you can also use your mini vacuum cleaner or the hose attachment for your regular vacuum to groom your pet. (This is probably not something you'd want to spring on an elderly pet with a heart problem, unless you know kitty or doggy CPR.)

Try using a child-size broom and mop for gathering the hair balls that accumulate between vacuumings.

A slightly damp sponge works great for removing hairs from upholstered furniture at a moment's notice. You can also use the bottom of a very clean sneaker that has ribbed soles for cleaning furniture.

During shedding season, besides combing or brushing your pet often, check your air conditioner and furnace filters frequently. They can become clogged with hair, making the system run inefficiently.

Litter boxes   To make litter box maintenance easier, do yourself a favor and use the newer, clumping-type litter. It costs a bit more, but it's worth it. Remove clumps and stools daily. (Cats are fastidious and eventually will skip the box if it gets too disgusting.) When cleaning, tip the litter box to one side to expose urine clumps and remove them whole. Do not shake them, or else you will mix dirty pieces with clean litter.

If you use regular kitty litter, clean the tray by emptying it and filling it with a half inch of vinegar. Let the vinegar stand for a few hours if you can. Dump out the vinegar, dry, and then dust the bottom with baking soda. Cover this with a layer of newspaper. This technique will control odors wonderfully.

Odors   You can give your smelly pet a quick dry bath by rubbing handfuls of baking soda or cornmeal into her fur, and brushing it out. Most smells should dissipate.

To eliminate skunk smell, the well-known tomato juice trick works best. Wash the animal with tomato juice, then rinse with a mixture of equal parts vinegar and water.

Urine   For dog urine, blot it up as soon after the accident as possible, then wash with a solution of ¼ teaspoon dishwashing liquid and 1 cup lukewarm water. Dampen the stain with a mixture of equal parts vinegar or lemon juice and water, then blot. Dampen with club soda and blot again.

This method works for cats, too, but you should also rub the spot with a cloth dampened with a bit of ammonia. The point is to eliminate the smell completely, because cats are prone to return to the scene of the crime.

For more on pet messes, see pages 88 and 92.

AQUARIUMS

If fish are your pets of choice, you can clean your aquarium with non-iodized salt and a heavy-duty plastic pot scrubber.

If algae have stained your coral, shells, or other aquarium toys, soak them in a weak solution of bleach and water, then rinse well under running water. Next soak them for at least 24 hours in aquarium water chlorine remover. Use a plastic basin or clean wastebasket for this purpose.

You can also clean coral with denture tablets, rinsing very well before putting them back in the aquarium.

Use caution with any cleaning product that might harm the fish — soap, detergent, ammonia, or bleach. Make sure you rinse items thoroughly if you use one of these products.

Keeping your tank out of direct sunlight will reduce algae buildup.

How to Shower with a Cat

For the truly committed pet owner, we offer this
proven method for de-fleaing your feline.

Does your cat have fleas? Every read the instructions on a flea shampoo bottle?

1. Wet cat. (Already you know you're in trouble.)
2. Put shampoo on cat. (Uh-huh. This would be a declawed cat, we presume.)
3. Leave shampoo on cat for 20 minutes. (Obviously, these instructions were written by a dog owner.)

One cat owner we know took on the cat/flea challenge this way. Her home was equipped with a large shower stall encased by sliding glass doors. Her cat was declawed. She read the label on the shampoo, determined there was nothing in it harmful to humans, and decided to shower with her cat.

After locking the cat in the bathroom, she disrobed, nabbed kitty and the bottle of shampoo, stepped into the shower, and closed the door. By the time the water was running, the cat was cornered. The caterwauling began, but at least in his terror, the poor thing wouldn't move from the farthest back corner. He merely cowered, shook, glared, and yowled as the shampoo was applied.

With 20 minutes to pass before she could rinse and release the cat, she showered herself, shaved, and shampooed – all to the sound of the yowling. To rinse, she took the showerhead and aimed it high above the cat, so that it rained a gentle shower down on him.

The yowls of terror are still talked about in that neighborhood, but the fleas haven't been seen since. The cat has recently begun holding his head up again in public, and the woman's daughter delights in telling people that her mother showers with cats.

*J*UST WHEN YOU THINK YOU HAVE A HANDLE ON ALL THE housework inside your house, you go outside and find out there's dirt out there, too! Although a topic such as cleaning the garage requires its own book, here are some tips for parts of the garage, the car that may or may not fit in it, and things attached to the outside of your house. Do these tasks when you need an excuse to be outside but still have the urge to be productive.

AROUND THE HOUSE

Canvas awnings   Remove the bird droppings on your canvas awnings by rubbing
a wire brush over a bar of naphtha soap
(available at hardware stores), then
scrubbing the spots and hosing them
down.

Concrete floors   There are many
variations on the theme of cleaning oil
spots from your driveway or concrete
garage floor. Here are a couple of solutions.
    Dampen the spot with water, then sprinkle with
heavy-duty laundry or dishwasher detergent. Scrub with a
stiff-bristle broom, then rinse with water.
    Try pouring on paint thinner, sprinkling with kitty litter, and cover-
ing the area with a damp cloth. Let sit for three to four hours, uncover,
and let dry before brushing away.
    Baking soda and cornmeal may take the oil out of concrete. Sprinkle
on, let dry, and sweep or vacuum away.
    Automotive and hardware stores sell a variety of commercial
products for removing oil spots from your garage floor. We haven't tried
them all, but one we did try was costly, highly toxic, and totally ineffec-
tive. Caveat emptor.

Indoor-outdoor carpeting   Clean indoor-outdoor carpeting by vacuuming thoroughly. Spray spots and other problem areas with a laundry
prewash treatment and let sit for 10 to 15 minutes. Wash down (using a
garden hose if drainage allows) and let dry. Or use a wet vac to pick up
most of the water, then let dry.

Siding   If you have aluminum or vinyl siding on your house, clean
it once a year with a strong spray from a hose. If some spots remain,
sponge them off with a solution of ¼ cup dishwashing liquid and
2 gallons water. Don't use anything abrasive, as this may damage
the siding.

Windows   What you use to clean your windows in your next spring-cleaning binge is perhaps less important than how and when you clean them (although we do suggest our HomeMade Glass Cleaner on page 113).

Don't do it when it's sunny and very hot. The cleaner will dry too quickly for you to control streaking.

When you're washing both inside and out, use horizontal strokes on one side and vertical strokes on the other. That way, if you see streaks afterward, you'll be able to tell which side they're on.

To make cleaning outside windows easier, use a spray bottle attachment (like those used to apply pesticides) on your hose. Fill the bottle with a solution of 1 teaspoon liquid dishwasher detergent and water. Spray windows lightly with the solution, scrub (wearing rubber gloves, as the detergent is harsh), and rinse with plain water.

Screens   Removing screens to clean them makes the job easier in the long run. To simplify the task, make a screen-cleaning station. Spread an old blanket or quilt on a flat outdoor surface (such as the driveway or picnic table). This keeps screens from stretching as you wash them. Place a

screen on the blanket and scrub with a soft brush using our HomeMade General-Purpose Cleaner (page 43) or (for really dirty screens) our HomeMade Heavy-Duty Disinfectant Cleaner (page 51). Stand the screen up and rinse it with your garden hose sprayer set to deliver a fine spray. Shake off the majority of the water, replace the screen in the window, and move on to the next screen. A two-person team will make this job go a lot faster.

EXTERIOR PAINTING

Before painting, dig your fingernails into a bar of soap and rub petroleum jelly into your hands or any other exposed skin that's likely to get spattered with paint. This will make your personal cleanup easier after a day of painting.

You can also protect yourself by wearing a plastic garbage bag while working (that is, if you don't have clothes that have been around since the Kennedy administration that you keep just for painting). Cut three holes in the bag, one for your head and one on each side for your arms. Use a disposable shower cap to cover your hair.

Protecting some surfaces while you paint will make both the painting and the cleanup go smoothly. Cover locks, hinges, and other metal hardware that you have to paint around with petroleum jelly. If you accidentally hit them with your paintbrush, the paint won't stick.

Do not try to apply paint to a mildewed surface. Mildew is anaerobic and will eat its way through the paint. Instead, clean the surface with our HomeMade Mildew Remover (page 52), then paint.

Brushes   Paintbrushes require special attention to keep them pliable and in good shape. One way to remove paint without getting harsh solvents such as turpentine on your hands is to put the brush in a self-sealing plastic sandwich bag with enough solvent to cover the bristles. Close the bag and squeeze the solvent through the brush. When you're finished, pour the solvent into a safe, sealed container and mark it clearly. You can use it again.

Vinegar makes a good paint solvent and keeps brushes pliable. You can do the plastic sandwich bag trick described above, using hot vinegar instead of turpentine or another solvent.

To soften natural-bristle brushes, add some liquid fabric softener to the final rinse of the brush.

Drips & spills   If you spill enamel paint, clean it up immediately with a soft, wet towel and some pumice soap (see page 128). Dried spatters of any paint on tile or windows can be removed with nail polish remover.

WASHING THE CAR

To begin with, make sure your rag, sponge, or brush is clean. Any dirt or sand lurking in your cleaning tool can easily scratch your car's finish. (If you do scratch the finish, find a crayon that matches the car's paint, rub it over the scratch, and buff with a clean cloth.)

Don't wash or wax your car in bright sunlight, as this may leave streaks.

Use only a mild dishwashing liquid to wash your car. (Dishwasher and laundry detergents can be too hard on your car's finish.) Or use a cleaner especially designed for cars.

If you really love your car's finish, after washing dry it with a soft, clean cloth to prevent spotting (especially if your town's or city's water is chlorinated).

To remove dead bugs from your grille or other areas, use a baking soda paste and a nylon scrubber. This does the trick without scratching the finish. (A baking soda paste also is good for polishing small nicks and scratches in your car's finish.)

You can remove tar by covering it with boiled linseed oil or vegetable oil, then rubbing with a soft cloth. You can also use mayonnaise or WD-40 to remove tar. Whatever you use, let it sit for a few minutes to soften the tar before rubbing.

Battery terminals   If you ever have to jump-start your car, you'll appreciate clean battery terminals. Scrub them with a paste of baking soda and water, then rub with petroleum jelly to keep them from corroding in the future.

BUMPER STICKER TRICK

Next time you apply a bumper sticker, remove only part of the protective backing. This will make it easier to take off the sticker when the time comes — and it will.

Bumper stickers   Tired of that "I like Ike" bumper sticker? You can remove it by heating it with a hair dryer, then lifting up one corner with a sharp knife to peel it off.

Another way to remove bumper stickers is to soak them

with nail polish remover, lighter fluid, or another solvent. Let the solvent sit long enough to loosen the glue, then peel the sticker off.

Carpet   Vacuum your car's carpet often to reduce wear and tear. As with carpeting inside your house, dirt and sand wear down the fibers every time you step on it. A hand-held, rechargeable vacuum is fine for light surface cleaning, but you need strong suction to get grit from deep in the pile, so use your regular vacuum cleaner for this. If you have an old (or spare) vacuum, put it in the garage near the car, plugged in and ready to go, so that you'll remember to clean the car occasionally.

Clean up spills on your car's carpet immediately (unless you *like* the smell of sour milk as you commute to work). Carry a roll of paper towels in your car and use them to blot up as much of the spill as possible. Refer to the section on page 83 for tips on cleaning up specific spills.

Remove road salt stains from your car's carpet with a mixture of up to equal parts vinegar and water. Work the solution into the carpet, then rinse thoroughly with water.

Chrome   Keep any chrome on your car waxed to prevent rust. If rust should occur, use the finest-grade (0000) steel wool to remove it.

Rubber floor mats   To make grungy rubber floor mats look like new, apply liquid shoe polish after washing them.

Windows   This one sounds obvious, but you can use windshield washer fluid to wash all your car's windows. Keep some in a spray bottle (well labeled), spray it on, wipe, and buff dry.

If the wipers are making marks on your windshield, wipe them with a baby wipe. (Keep these in your car for cleaning hands, faces, and minor spills while traveling.)

On a new car, remove the price sticker sheets by soaking them with vinegar or salad oil, then peeling them off.

Chapter 10
Odds & Ends

OU'VE JUST BOUGHT THE CRUISE TICKETS AND DISCOVER that your luggage, last used at Boy Scout camp, smells like your son's socks.

The new puppy had his first accident on your toddler's favorite teddy bear.

Company's coming, and your peacock feathers are looking dingy.

The answers to these cleaning conundrums can be found here, along with tips for a lot of other stuff you're not sure how to clean.

CLEANING HINTS

Artificial flowers   Clean the dust that collects on your silk flowers by washing them in a basin of cool water with a few drops of a mild liquid laundry detergent (the kind made for hand-washing delicates) added. If the flowers are made of fabric, dust them by using your blow dryer set on low, or place them in a paper bag with ¼ cup salt. Close the bag and shake.

Barbecue grills   Lawn and garden stores that sell barbecue grills have many tools for cleaning them, but one of the best tools we've discovered is a pumice stone specifically shaped for that purpose. (This is especially good if you lack upper body strength.)

You may try to loosen hardened-on crud with dishwasher detergent or oven cleaner (either a commercial product or our HomeMade Oven Cleaner on page 41). Squirt or spray on the cleaner, place the grill in a large plastic garbage bag, seal, and let sit for several hours or overnight. Then scrub (a grill scrubber with a handle works well for this) and rinse very well.

If you have a gas grill, try cooking the crud off by covering the grill with foil, turning the gas on high and closing the lid. This should burn off the crud in 10 minutes.

GUNK BE GONE

To avoid having too much stuck-on gunk, spray your grill with nonstick cooking spray. It'll make future cleanups easier.

Baskets   If you're one who uses a lot of baskets for decorating and holding things, you know how dusty and dirty they can get. Never soak a basket. Vacuum it with the upholstery brush attachment. If further cleaning is needed, wipe it with a damp cloth and dry immediately with a dry cloth.

If mildew is a problem, combine 1 tablespoon bleach and ¼ cup hot water, apply to a cloth, scrub the basket, and dry well.

Books   A home is not a home without books (in our opinion), but having them on the shelf also means plenty of places for dust to accumulate and, worse, for mold and mildew to grow. If dust is your only challenge, take the books off the shelf one at a time and vacuum them with the upholstery brush attachment. You can also wipe them with a dust rag. If you have old, leather-bound books, clean the bindings with saddle soap. Be sure to dry them well.

Remove mildew from hardback book covers with our HomeMade Heavy-Duty Disinfectant Cleaner (page 51) or a weak solution of vinegar and water. Apply sparingly and blot dry immediately. (If you have valuable texts in your collection, it's best to consult a professional for mold and mildew control, especially since mold can spread to other books.)

You can get price stickers off books and book jackets without damaging them by setting your iron on low to medium heat and using a pressing cloth. Press over the sticker for a few seconds to loosen the glue, then peel it off.

Candles   If your candles have become dusty, clean them with a cloth dipped in a little denatured alcohol or liquid wax.

Candleholders   To remove wax from candleholders, run them under very hot water. Drips will rub off, and candle stubs should come out more easily.

For candleholders that shouldn't be immersed in water, place them in the freezer for an hour or more. The frozen wax will be easier to pick off.

UNSTICK THE STUBS

Candle stubs will come out of your candleholders more easily if you spray the inside of the holders with nonstick cooking spray before inserting a new candle.

Canvas tents   Clean the family tent by using our HomeMade General-Purpose Cleaner (page 43) with warm water and a scrub brush. If the tent is mildewed from being stored while damp, use our HomeMade Heavy-Duty Disinfectant Cleaner (page 51) or our HomeMade Mildew Remover (page 52), or wash down the tent with vinegar. Let it dry in the sun.

Ceiling tiles   To deal with marks on ceiling tiles, try erasing them with an art gum eraser or hiding them with white chalk. A dry eraser also works for this, if you can find one at a hardware or furniture store

Combs & brushes   Combs and brushes collect hair, oils, and buildup from shampoos and other hair care products. Clean them effectively by soaking them in a sinkful of water with 3 tablespoons baking soda and 3 tablespoons bleach.

 Wash hairbrushes with a teaspoonful or more of powdered borax dissolved in a pint of warm water, or with saleratus [baking soda] and water. (1871)

You can also soak brushes for 30 minutes in hot water with dishwashing liquid or shampoo. Then run a comb through them. Rinse each item thoroughly.

Stubborn gunk may be removed from combs with a bath of ammonia and water.

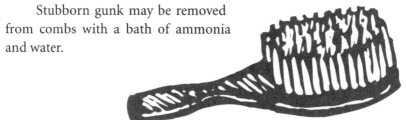

Dolls & stuffed animals   What kid doesn't have a favorite teddy bear or doll that's impossible to steal away for washing? A cloth doll can be washed using the gentle cycle of your machine, after you've removed all its clothing and other accessories. Put the doll in a pillowcase, knot the open end, and wash it with several towels. Dry briefly on low, then let dry overnight in a well-ventilated spot or outside in the sun all day.

Some stuffed animals (check the tag) may be washed this way as well.

Cornstarch may work as a dry shampoo for stuffed animals and cloth dolls. Rub it in, let it sit for an hour or so, and then brush or vacuum it off.

Eyeglasses   Clean plastic lenses according to the manufacturer's directions. Plastics vary, but all can be easily scratched. The worst thing you can do is clean plastic lenses with any product containing ammonia.

Clean glass lenses with alcohol and water, or hold them under running water and dab with a bit of dishwashing liquid.

A very dilute mixture of vinegar and water also works to clean glasses.

Save your empty dishwashing liquid
bottle, fill it with water, and shake it to make
a weak soap solution that's perfect for cleaning glasses.

If you've spattered paint on your glass lenses, carefully apply acetone or mineral spirits using a soft cloth. Rinse and dry thoroughly.

Feathers   If your biggest cleaning problem is the dust collecting in
your ostrich or peacock feathers, rest easy. You
can dust them with your hair dryer set
on low. If that doesn't leave the
feathers with that just-plucked
look, swish them in a bit of
cold water, then blow-
dry them on low.

Hair rollers   Hair rollers that have accumulated gunk can be cleaned
by soaking them in ½ cup vinegar and 1 cup water. Scrub the rollers with
a toothbrush and dry well.

Jewelry   For general cleaning, try our HomeMade Jewelry Cleaner
(page 148).

Diamonds   Diamond jewelry can be cleaned using white or clear dishwashing liquid in boiling water. Put the diamond in a strainer and dip it
in the soapy water for a few seconds, then soak it in alcohol for 10 seconds. Air-dry on tissue paper.

Gold
Gold ornaments, when plain or worked and unadorned with
gems, should always be washed in warm soapsuds from time to
time, excellent results being obtained if a few drops of sal volatile are added
to the hot water before making the lather. In the case of chains composed of
close links, which are most apt to harbor dirt and dust, few remedies equal
that of placing them to soak in a bottle half full of warm soapsuds mixed
with a little prepared chalk. (1915)

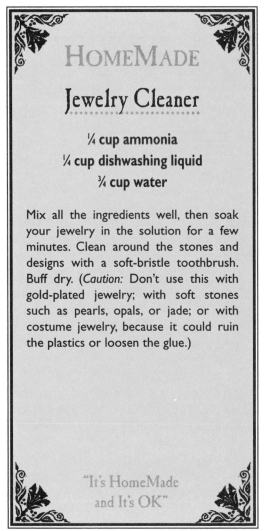

HomeMade

Jewelry Cleaner

¼ cup ammonia
¼ cup dishwashing liquid
¾ cup water

Mix all the ingredients well, then soak your jewelry in the solution for a few minutes. Clean around the stones and designs with a soft-bristle toothbrush. Buff dry. (*Caution:* Don't use this with gold-plated jewelry; with soft stones such as pearls, opals, or jade; or with costume jewelry, because it could ruin the plastics or loosen the glue.)

"It's HomeMade
and It's OK"

Pearls Clean pearls by swishing them in cold water. Dry them gently with a soft towel. Don't soak pearls, because this can damage the string.

Silver You can clean silver jewelry by coating it with a bit of toothpaste (not the gel type). Let the toothpaste sit for an hour or so, then rub it off with a dry cloth. This works best for smooth silver pieces or chains.

Labels, stickers & decals   To remove a sticky label or decal from an immersible item, soak it in warm, soapy water.

For a nonimmersible item, heat the sticker gently with a warm iron to loosen the glue, then peel it off. This trick also works well to remove tape from boxes and wrapping paper that you'd like to save.

To remove paper stuck to polished surfaces, soak with olive oil and then peel off.

Lamp chimney   Clean a kerosene lamp chimney by pouring a bit of kerosene on a piece of newspaper, rubbing the lamp with it, and wiping dry. Be sure the chimney is completely dry before lighting, and dispose of the newspaper in a closed container away from heat.

Louvered doors   A louvered door can present a special cleaning problem. There's hardly any tool available to clean between the slats efficiently. Try wrapping a thin terry cloth towel around a paint stick or yardstick. Dampen the cloth slightly or spray it with our HomeMade General-Purpose Cleaner (page 43), then slide the stick between the slats. If the door is small or extremely soiled, consider removing it from its hinges, as it'll be much easier to clean that way.

Luggage & trunks   Carpet or upholstery cleaner works well for cleaning nylon luggage. Try our HomeMade Rug Cleaner (page 85).

Plastic or vinyl luggage can be cleaned with our HomeMade General-Purpose Cleaner (page 43).

Leather luggage should be cleaned with saddle soap.

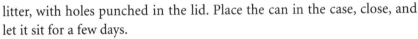

If you have musty-smelling luggage or travel trunks, put an open box of baking soda inside, close the case, and let it sit overnight or longer.

Another odor killer for luggage and trunks is a coffee can filled with kitty litter, with holes punched in the lid. Place the can in the case, close, and let it sit for a few days.

Model airplane glue   Generally, model airplane glue can be removed using acetone, except on acetate, Verel, and Dynel.

Another way to remove airplane glue is to soak the item in a solution of equal parts vinegar and boiling water. Boil until any stain is removed. Rinse with water.

Paintings   You should leave the cleaning of any valuable work of art to a professional, but you can dust an oil painting by brushing it with a soft, clean paintbrush reserved just for this purpose.

Piano keys   If piano keys have become yellowed, clean them with a mixture of a mild dishwashing liquid and water, wiping each key as you go with a slightly damp cloth. Rinse with a damp cloth, then dry each key thoroughly.

Denatured alcohol also works for cleaning piano keys, but don't use wax or abrasive cleansers on ivory.

If piano keys are stained, dampen a cloth and dip it in baking soda. Rub the stain with the soda, then wipe with a clean cloth and buff dry.

See page 96 for a tip on cleaning between keys.

Picture frames

 The white of an egg applied with a small camel hair brush will remove fly-traces and soil from gilt frames; or the water in which onions have been boiled will if rubbed over the frame, remove dust and specks and brighten the gilding. (1910)

If you'd rather not use egg whites or onion water to clean a gilt picture frame, clean it with equal parts ammonia and rubbing alcohol, applied with a small brush. Pat it dry.

Plants   Houseplants are living things that sometimes require attention to their personal hygiene.

Clean any plants with furry leaves (such African violets) with a soft brush, perhaps a toothbrush or watercolor brush. You can also dust the leaves with a feather duster.

For shiny-leaved plants, sprinkle glycerin on a cloth and swab them gently, or polish them with a mixture of equal parts milk and water. To prevent dust from collecting, spritz the leaves occasionally with water.

Rust   You can clean the rust from bicycle chains and other metal objects by soaking them in cola, which has a pH of about 2.6, halfway between coffee and hydrochloric acid. (Aside from the sugar content, this is why your mother always said your teeth would fall out if you drank too much of the stuff.)

See pages 77 and 88 for tips on cleaning rust stains on fabrics and carpets.

Shoes   A clever, quick shoe polisher is a banana peel. Rub the peel over the shoe and then buff with a clean cloth.

Another quick and easy shoeshine tool is a fabric softener sheet.

Clean the salt marks off your winter boots and shoes with a mixture of one part vinegar and three parts water.

A toothbrush works well to clean shoe treads clogged with mud or dirt. Keep one handy just for that purpose.

See page 66 for tips on cleaning sneakers.

Straw matting & hats   Woven mats of various kinds can be cleaned by dipping them in warm water with dishwashing liquid, then in clear water, and laying them between two towels to dry.

Here are two other suggestions for cleaning straw items.

 Straw matting may be cleaned with a large, coarse cloth dipped in salt and water and then wiped dry. The salt prevents the matting from turning yellow.

An old piece of velvet makes an excellent brush for a dark straw hat.

(1918)

Velcro   Velcro can pick up lint and fuzz that clogs it and renders it unusable. To clean Velcro, rub another piece of the same type of Velcro over it.

Wood stove steamer & large kettles   If your wood stove steamer or large kettles have white spots on them, the spots are probably lime deposits. To remove them, fill the item with water and add 2 tablespoons vinegar and a few lemon slices or some rhubarb. Boil for 15 minutes, then scrub the spots. Rinse and dry.

Index